OU Men

Work Through Lifelong Learning

Related book by the author: *OU Women: Undoing Educational Obstacles*, 1994. London: Cassell.

Patricia W. Lunneborg

OU Men

Work Through Lifelong Learning

The Lutterworth Press
Cambridge

First published in 1997 by

The Lutterworth Press

P.O. Box 60

Cambridge

CB1 2NT

British Library Cataloguing-in-Publication Data

A catalogue record for this book is available from the British Library.

ISBN 0 7188 2972 7

Cover photo by Mike Levers, OU Chief Photographer

Printed in the UK by
Redwood Books, Trowbridge, Wiltshire

Contents

Foreword

This is an inspiring and powerful book. Patricia Lunneborg explores the dilemmas of late 20th century Britain through the eyes and voices of a wonderfully diverse group of individuals. Almost the only thing these fifteen men have in common, apart from their gender, is that they have studied with The Open University. Ms Lunneborg's original intention was to find out how obtaining a degree later in life affected various aspects of men's lives: their leisure; their relationships; their values. But she quickly found that her subjects were inarticulate on such topics. Only when talking about the impact of continuing education on their careers did they really open up. So men, study and work are the focus of the book.

A highly effective structure makes the book as a whole more than the sum of its parts. The author interleaves the portraits that emerged from her meetings with fifteen OU men with short, telling chapters on Britain's contemporary working environment, drawing particularly on the work of Charles Handy, Will Hutton and Jeremy Rifkin. These link chapters explore the current trends in the labour market which are the root cause of the anxieties that led these men to protect their future by continuing their education. Jobs traditionally done by men are declining whilst those considered as women's work are multiplying. Not more than 40% of men —a core elite which includes most union members —now have full-time jobs with relative security. British levels of male job satisfaction are among Europe's lowest —and the incidence of job related illness among the highest. Large numbers of young men seem to have been born into obsolescence and cannot contemplate a normal family life. Yet, at the other end of the scale, the well-paid jobs of their successful contemporaries demand a culture of presenteeism where 60-hour weeks in the office also play havoc with human relationships.

Yet despite these depressing trends, and despite the accounts of grim workplaces and immoral employers, the stories of these OU men pack a tremendous punch of optimism and hope. I was touched by them at two levels. Touched first in my role as Vice-Chancellor. In presiding at dozens of OU degree ceremonies I have had conversations with thousands of graduates as I shake their hands on the stage. In their interviews with Pat Lunneborg these men confirm my own impression of the overwhelmingly positive impact of OU study on people's lives and provide wonderful detail on exactly how it helped them. Second, I found these stories inspiring in purely personal terms. All men, even those whose careers have been a succession of fulfilling jobs, worry about their next move and about what they will do in retirement. For me these fifteen case histories were uplifting and encouraging. Their common theme is that continuing study helps you face uncertainty with equanimity.

The book gains from being written by an American woman. As an American, Pat Lunneborg views the British working environment with fresh eyes. She pauses and explores aspects of working life which a British male author would have taken for granted. Being a woman, she in fact achieves her original aim of documenting how OU study wove itself into the rich tapestries of her subjects' lives. Starting with descriptions of where each interview took place and what each man was wearing, she paints a living portrait that allows her readers to feel that we have met these graduates too — and found them, as she did, `nice men, gentle men and thoughtful men'.

The men shared a common approach to OU study. All reported the need for determination, for taking charge of themselves, for setting targets, and for focus. They found it better to study at a steady pace and get good marks than to undertake several courses at once. The support of partners is invaluable — lack of it a real obstacle. In a number of cases spouses and other family members were also OU students. Comments about the context and purpose of study revealed greater variety. Some chose subjects linked to their job. Others, like the actor who opted for science because it was dispassionate, wanted something completely different. Some talked about their studies at work while others kept them secret.

There are many similarities in the benefits these OU men attribute to their degrees. All gained in confidence and self-esteem. They felt like winners. Universal also was the belief that study had made them more adaptable and broadened the scope of their lives. For a number the OU degree was a route to promotion, job enhancement or a career change — often from a traditionally male job into the service sector. Over the years of study most changed their circle of friends as the OU brought them contact with a wider cross section of society. The nature of their relationships evolved and they became more discerning about people. One graduate realised, without regret, that he was no longer `one of the lads' and found, to his surprise, that he could develop ordinary friendships with women.

Most of the men told Pat Lunneborg that after OU study it was almost a reflex to see different sides of any question. They report a growing interest in knowledge for its own sake, a new ability to co-operate in the sharing of ideas, and increased confidence as public speakers. As well as giving greater job satisfaction, the OU degree led some to become more involved in community activities — perhaps because the end of OU study was an anti-climax and they had to build up their social lives again.

What are the lessons for the OU itself? Those men with experience of other universities found the OU better and more demanding. Clearly the OU is now providing teachers of postgraduate courses in other universities with some very critical customers! While opinions of tutorials vary, all who commented said their OU tutors were the cornerstone of the system. For several men some encouraging comments from a tutor on their early work had a dramatic effect on their determination to succeed. Some of those interviewed derived great enjoyment from summer schools and various OU student clubs.

I urge any man who is feeling anxious about work or retirement to browse in this book. Browsing will lead you to read it from cover to cover, for these inspiring stories contain some wonderful vignettes of modern life. Three of my favourites were:

Category 1. OU study is more fun than work:

"I have to read standing up in my room because some of the stuff is so damned boring" (aircraft manuals not OU units!).

Category 2. Summer school leads to a new marriage:

"I took this seven-ton truck from Wigan down to Romsey and loaded up Susan's stuff with her husband looking on. It was a funny day, that."

Category 3. Withdrawal pains after an OU course:

"When I'd finished and done the exam, I was getting up in the night and going down to the kitchen to do calculus as a relaxing, mental exercise. It's almost the same kind of pleasure you get from a good coffee."

Sir John Daniel, Vice-Chancellor, The Open University

Acknowledgements

The person who has helped me the most with this book is my partner, Clifford Lunneborg, Permanent Visiting Research Professor in the Department of Statistics, The Open University. He accompanied me on my travels, taught me Word 7.0, and picked out the photo for the cover. But his primary help was emotional support whenever I needed it, and, believe me, writers need a lot of it.

My heartfelt thanks to Sir John Daniel for a sterling Foreword. And heartfelt thanks as well to David Grugeon, the OU's Director of UK Partnerships, for believing in the worth of the project. Also I'm indebted to Annette Mathias, OU Press Officer, who supplied me with lists of graduates who agreed to be contacted for publicity purposes. I appreciate the enthusiastic support for the project from Giles Clark, OU Deputy Managing Editor, Book Trade, and from Tia Downer, Administrative Officer of the Association of Open University Graduates (AOUG). And last, but not least, Tanja Howarth, my agent, gets credit for the idea of following up OU Women with OU Men.

I also acknowledge here that I take full responsibility for any discrepancies and errors which have crept into the men's stories. One disadvantage to the American observer of the British scene is accents. Especially when the interviewee gets excited and starts speaking rapidly, so that months later, back in America, the interviewer plays the tape over and over to her husband and they play a game of `Sounds to me like....'

Preface

This book documents a brilliant way out, for fifteen individuals, of this Age of Uncertainty for men. The men are not CEOs, not drivers of multinational conglomerates, nor executives in great institutions. They are ordinary guys living ordinary lives, which means like all men today they are confronted with a confusing, rapidly changing world of work. New ideas of full- and part-time. New ideas about unemployment, retirement, absenteeism. New ideas about various forms of work—paid, gift, home, and study. In fact, it is this last form of work, study, which is the way out for these men.

Like my last book, *OU Women: Undoing Educational Obstacles*, to which this book is a kind of sequel, the stories are tied together with brief commentary on work and lifelong learning. I had a quite different concept when I started the project. I was going to focus on how a university degree, aside from benefiting a man's job prospects, affected his emotional life, recreational life, interests, values, and needs. Well, that idea didn't work very well. In the interviews the men kept coming back to what was the centre of their lives—indeed, most men's lives—jobs. Questions about relationships, sex roles, and housework produced a lot of hemming and hawing. But about their careers, they couldn't tell me enough. So the book is about work and, most importantly, how continued adult learning keeps a man in work.

Except for Steven Tharpe, whom I already knew, the men's names were provided by Annette Mathias, Open University Press Officer, from lists of OU graduates of 1993-94 who had agreed to be contacted about their educational experiences. I did the first interview in February 1994 and the last in February 1995. We met in various settings, where they worked or were currently studying, in their home or mine. The nonconfidential interviews lasted two hours and were taped.

Who's this book for? Men who are frustrated, angry and frightened about the workplace changes that threaten their status, earnings, security, and sense of self-worth. Men who want illustrations of how one strategy for coping with the Age of Uncertainty—going back to school—operates and why it is successful. Men who'd like examples of how to get greater control over their lives. Men who are eager not to lose everything that can go out the window when you lose your job.

Some of the men I talked with came from very limited educational backgrounds, yet they succeeded. Several are from ethnic and racial minorities which compounds the problems faced by white Anglo-Saxon males, yet they succeeded. All, however, were motivated to try higher education as the solution to their mounting anxieties about the future. Their hard-earned degrees answered their needs, and then some. The book proceeds as follows.

Chapter 1, Age of Uncertainty, presents the dilemma for men of a work environment daily shedding traditional male jobs and calling for more flexibility from, and less security for, workers. It also introduces my three main resources, the books *The Age of Unreason, The State We're In,* and *The End of Work.* Finally, the way out of this age of hopelessness is proposed—ever-increasing knowledge.

Jim Bailey, Chapter 2, shifted from computer services to human resources within Marathon Petroleum, thanks to his bachelor's degree. Redundancy is no longer perceived as a fearful, full stop to career, but as a challenge to use his greater confidence and hard-won systems approach to tackle any problem.

Chapter 3, Job Dissatisfaction As the Norm, explores the causes of the pervasive feel-bad factor in the workplace, especially for men. Even the male managers doing the downsizing and job-redefining have record levels of stress due to increased workloads, longer hours, unreasonable deadlines, and no time for partners or hobbies or even looking after themselves.

Lawry Rhodes' midlife transition from a co-opted building society manager to English teacher is detailed in Chapter 4. His greater self-confidence also has led to work as an actor, director, and poet.

Chapter 5, Stress of Presenteeism, concerns the increased workloads and extra hours demanded of the workers left behind after restructuring. Many of the jobs hardest hit by stress are `men's jobs', and the job levels hardest hit are men's as well.

Every university course that Lamber Dosanjh in Chapter 6 took was over unfamiliar territory. But with his foresight, every course had to do with computers. So when BT computerized itself—with Lamber's job changing every year—he was able to teach himself and keep his position despite massive downsizing.

Chapter 7, Stress of Obsolescence, is about male joblessness, the waste of younger, undereducated men, now suiciding at unprecedented levels, and of educated, experienced older men, being passed over so that 40-year-old elite high flyers can run the country's corporations.

Steven Barker in Chapter 8 describes how he went from redundancy as a paint technician to the challenges of a qualified social worker. One challenge being, what do you say to an adolescent coming out of long-term care who sees stealing as work, the only way he can find pride in himself?

Chapter 9, Age of the Skills Portfolio, declares that a resume with only one or two jobs in it won't get you very far in today's skills market. It challenges older generations to stay in the classroom because `not getting smarter is getting dumber.'

George Saint of Chapter 10 is an extraordinary East Ender whose university degree won him a manager's job with London Underground. However, should that end, he can be a very educated lorry driver, Class I, anywhere in the world.

Chapter 11, Age of Early Retirement, says that retirement in one's 50s will soon belong only to a core elite of knowledgeable professionals. The rest of the work force, contracted, part-time, temporary, will be working past 65. The solution? Reinforce your portfolio with many varieties of work.

Mahmood Tootoonchian of Chapter 12 turned to the OU in retirement to develop himself and earn a degree in psychology. He now translates, studies, enjoys the Iranian community of London, and continues to feel like a winner.

Chapter 13, A Crisis in Men's Health, documents that Britain's workers are the sick men of Europe. Too much employment is as bad for men as too little. How to get men to take care of themselves is the question.

To illustrate how knowledge might make men look after their physical and emotional health is the story of nurse, Michael Moore, of Chapter 14. Michael's well-being is centered in a portfolio of always-expanding computer expertise, a stable, long-term relationship, a comfortable house in a small town, and lots of sunshine holidays.

Chapter 15 is titled The State We're In For and lays out Will Hutton's 30/30/40 society in which only 40 per cent of workers are full-time employees. More downsizing and corporate restructuring are on the way. But as Chapter 15 is a transition chapter, three forward-looking solutions are proposed, starting with a shorter workweek.

Commercial pilot Peter Bolton in Chapter 16 is a premier example of a fifty-year-old whose OU degree gave him the confidence to leave a treadmill job and search for something better. He also testifies to an ironic benefit of distance learning—meeting and studying with many different people—`In them you see it is possible to change.'

Chapter 17, Education As The Answer, quotes Willy Russell, Paddy Ashdown, Sir John Daniel, Charles Handy, to the effect that if you want to be in control of your change, take learning seriously, no matter how old you are.

Then comes Tony Osmond, Chapter 18, whose OU experience gave him a new wife, a new life, and a new job. Even though it's `just a job', his totally calmed down personality means he now enjoys good relationships with his workmates.

Chapter 19, Future Job Security says an individual's skills and knowledge are the only security left. Close upon us is a world where most people's identities will no longer reside in paid employment, but in work in the Third Sector, unpaid community service.

Rajesh Ragiwala of Chapter 20, a BT commercial officer promoted since his honours BA, illustrates future employment security through his expanded portfolio and serious investment planning with his partner for the worst financial scenarios. Conveniently, Raj already has a built-in community to contribute to.

Chapter 21, More Time for Home Work, pleads for men who face shorter workweeks, if they have employment at all, to devote more time to `home work', the most important of which is caring for children, the elderly, neighbors.

The only house husband in the bunch, Eugene MacLaughlin from Northern Ireland, in Chapter 22 details his career change from teaching business studies to becoming a lawyer by way of a politics and economics OU degree.

Chapter 23, More Time for Gift Work, warns that unless voluntary community service is organised to rebuild communities, we are doomed to crime and violence and a vast outlaw culture.

Land surveyor, Sam Ampem in Chapter 24, tells of his struggles to balance his study of mathematics with his counselling activities among needy Ghanian refugees. He will certainly use his counselling skills as much as his math studies when he shifts from surveying to teaching today's troubled teenagers.

Chapter 25, New Ideas about Work, pushes nontraditional, `women's jobs' for men. Teaching, nursing, social work, secretarial work, while underpaid and stressful, cannot be eliminated by technology. Women's jobs are the last preserve of a `job for life'.

In Chapter 26 we meet David Gildner, now challenged by multiple sclerosis, who went from being an illiterate factory worker to being a poet and activities organiser at a daycare centre for the elderly. Once David's OU qualifications were on his resume, career change was his for the asking.

Chapter 27, Lifelong Learning, hints at the many opportunities for lifelong learning besides the Open University—accelerated courses at new universities, The Open College, corporate training, postgraduate studies. A third of people in all age groups should be entering higher education to meet the UK's need for intelligent workers and it isn't happening.

A scientist who got diverted by language studies and an acting career, Ian Flintoff in Chapter 28 describes studying chemistry, physics, and biology with the OU and gives us his ideas as to when people should be educated.

Last but not least, Stephen Tharpe describes a most creative and fulfilling retirement in Chapter 29 where he puts into practice Charles Handy's idea that older people who leave their professions should return as assistants to the next generation.

Chapter 30, The End of Work?, summarizes the triumph of these fifteen men over downsizing, presenteeism, early reduncancy, and outsourcing. If you want to stay in the core elite, you must stay in education—that's one message. Another message is that we've all got to get involved in unpaid `gift work' as we enter a future of global markets, automated production, and near-workerless economies.

I learned so much from this project. Most important that continuing education makes very nice men. Gentle men, thoughtful men, effusive optimistic men, men who went back to school for their careers' sakes and learned to love learning for its own sake. They discovered there are other things far more important than their jobs; they became planners, dreamers, lifelong learners, and believers that they can survive, even thrive, no matter what comes their way. They have learned calm and confidence facing the Age of Uncertainty and it made them altogether delightful to get to know.

Chapter 1

Age of Uncertainty

> Organised religion on the defensive, trade unions
> emasculated, the National Health Service a two-tier structure,
> public sector employees poorly rewarded, education a creator
> of class division.... These changes have affected the deepest
> parts of the British psyche. The notion of a fair day's work for
> a fair day's pay, the idea that success will attend hard work
> and that society should support basic institutions like
> families and children— all are evaporating. Individuals are
> compelled to look out for themselves.... Jobs can be lost
> quickly and never found again; lifetime savings can be stolen;
> home buyers can be trapped by debt in houses worth less
> than the price paid for them. There is a general sense of fear
> and beleaguerment (Hutton, pp.9-10).

How fifteen men coped with `all of the above' is what this book is about. Among them is a paint technician made redundant who had no other skills to rely on. Also, two men who retired `early' to become qualified for second careers, only to fall prey to age discrimination. And a freelance black surveyor whose sporadic contracts forced him to rethink job security and job satisfaction.

You will meet a pilot tired of traveling long distances by car to get to his job, and a semi-skilled machine operator whose rage over factory conditions rendered him speechless. There are two British Telecom employees who watched thousands be laid off while they held on to jobs that now change completely at least once a year. And there's a building society manager whose position was secure as long as he blackmailed customers into policies that were no good to them at all.

What the men did—to train for new careers, keep the jobs they had, become qualified for promotion, move horizontally within an organisation, or develop after-work identities—was to continue their education. They pursued university degrees and in the process became advocates of lifelong learning. I, too, believe strongly in never-ending education and so we got together to put their success stories in print.

My main resources in this project, in addition to the men themselves, are three books, Charles Handy's (1995a) *The Age of Unreason*, Will Hutton's (1996) *The State We're In*, and Jeremy Rifkin's (1995) *The End of Work*. They document the Age of Uncertainty as well as anyone and I quote them so frequently, I will omit repeating these publication dates. I urge you to read all three books, but, *but*—their writing is not directed at individuals so much as governments, industries, and organisations. I'll give you briefly their main points but I leave the bulk of my book to the men in the belief that the more *they* say to you, the more you'll learn about lifelong learning.

So, what's happening? Job layoffs continue to dominate the business pages. Burn-out and the stresses of presenteeism plague those who aren't let go as they try to work twice as hard to make up for lost colleagues. Survivors suffer the gnawing fear of the next downsizing and do without promotions and raises which were the custom not too very long ago. Those retained are also required to get with the new technologies and if they can't, they're gone.

The service sector is growing, the manufacturing sector is disappearing. Short-term contracts are expanding, salaried employees are a thing of the past. Temporary is the vogue, permanent is not. Do-it-yourself health, disability, and pension benefits are in, company benefits are out. That pretty well sums it up. Except for the elderly we are shocked to see behind the counter at the news agent's, sweeping the streets, and selling popcorn at the cinema. Why are they still working? How many victims did Robert Maxwell have?

De-scaling, re-designing, restructuring, rationalising, re-engineering, delayering, delevelling, core re-emphasising, unassigning. Generation X may lap it up, but the rest of us could use some help.

The rise of women's work, the decline of manufacturing

Women's jobs have expanded over the past two decades while traditional male jobs have disappeared. More women than men work in service industries, more men than women work in manufacturing. Manufacturing jobs are going, service jobs are growing. So you can't really say that women are taking men's jobs.

Women will work part-time while men think it's beneath them. In the UK the increase in employment since the economic `recovery' began has come entirely through part-time jobs. And around the world part-time work is on the rise, but in no country does more than one man in ten do it. Again, it's easy to see why the new jobs in Britain go to women. But women are not driving men from the workplace (The war between the sexes, 1994).

Manufacturing firms now employ only one worker in five in the UK. The decline of jobs in manufacturing since 1970 has been steeper in Britain than in Germany, Japan, France, and the US, dropping from 37% to 20%, while service jobs went from 50% to 73%. `Service' isn't simply flipping hamburgers. It's everything that isn't manufacturing: stockbroking, office work, selling, banking, local government, science, public service, real estate. Service includes most high-level, knowledge-based jobs, *needing far more education than manufacturing jobs* (The manufacturing myth, 1994).

How corporations stay `competitive'

A big reason behind the instability of the job market is that to stay quote unquote competitive, businesses now follow a formula that says the way to Productivity and Profit is: Half the people paid double, working twice as hard and producing three times as much. These high flyers will be referred to throughout this book as the core elite. All other workers are on contract, or, worse, on call as part-time, temporary slavies brought in as needed, then dispensed with until the next crisis.

Is there a way out?

Yes. One way out is knowledge. Going back to college and staying there. Handy opines that intellectual property, the brains and know-how of a workforce, has replaced physical property—land and raw materials—as the measure of a nation's wealth. What that means for the individual is that he must go after education as avidly as the men of yesteryear went after land.

The Age of Unreason starts by saying, `Today we know that in many areas of life we cannot guarantee more of the same, be it work or money, peace or freedom, health or happiness, and cannot even predict with confidence what will be happening in our own lives. Change is now more chancy, but also more exciting if we want to see it that way.'

These men no longer see change as threatening. They are convinced that the more you study, the better chance you have of paid work. At the same time, the more understanding you acquire, the less important is success at any job. Because with the confidence of a lifelong learner, you will always be `in work' .

The time is looming when most men will only work for pay part-time. To thrive in this age men must embrace other, unpaid forms of work, at home, in education, in the community. How do they do that? We'll start with Jim Bailey, my first interviewee back in February 1994. Marathon Petroleum had the decency to warn Jim of what it would take to survive in its future, know-how. He took their advice and got far more out of it than a promotion.

Chapter 2

Jim Bailey, Marathon Man

Why did I succeed? It was partly being pushed by my wife, and partly Marathon management saying, `A degree would be a definite advantage.' Then studying took on a life of its own and I thought, I'm doing this for me. At the end of the first year, I thought, My God, I've got five years to go, but I'll stick with it. It became a personal goal. Even if I'd failed a couple of exams, I would have continued. And that was an aspect of me that I wasn't aware of, this determination to finish.

Jim Bailey came down the open staircase into the lobby of Marathon Petroleum in regulation executive garb—grey suit, white shirt, a bright, blazing tropical tie. Well, the tie was probably more Jim than regulation. We did our interview in a seminar room with its large polished mahogony table, slide projector and flip charts, the only decoration stark photographs of glittering drilling platforms rising out of icy waters.

Jim, who was raised in a working class family in Manchester, has been with Marathon for fourteen years. He's gone into human resources from computer services and been a HR representative for the past four years. Julie, his wife of sixteen years, is a legal secretary. Jim is 41 and began the OU when he was 34. He left school with eight O-levels, no A-levels.

Your reasons for doing a university degree?

I'd recently been promoted into a supervisory position and I was discussing career progression with my manager. One of the things he mentioned was further education to degree level. So I said I'll do it and I went through the big Open University newspaper, looked at the courses, picked out the one that I thought I would struggle least with, Living with Technology.

What obstacles did you have?

As a youngster I didn't enjoy school and the atmosphere at the time was there were a lot more jobs around and people tended to leave and go to work. It wasn't considered essential to have any further education. If you went to university then, it was because you were particularly interested in some subject, or because you wanted a career that required a degree. My main interest was getting out of school as quickly as possible and earning money so I could go out and enjoy myself.

In the junior school, higher years, I was resentful of all the discipline. That was a bugbear. There were times when I was doing a subject that I enjoyed, and because the boys around me were causing a disturbance, I'd get lumped in with them. I used to think, why couldn't they ask, were you involved? It was just, `Out!' They'd send us to the headmaster who'd shout at us or you'd get a rap over the knuckles. I most enjoyed English and art, although I wasn't particularly talented.

How have your studies changed you?

Its main effect is greater self-esteem. It has made me a lot more confident. If I'm in a meeting with a number of highly qualified engineering staff, I feel on a par. We've all qualified in further education. I can't say I had an inferiority complex before, but it has made me feel a lot easier with people. I moved into the HR Department when I was about a third of the way through the degree.

My approach to thinking is different now. The course I did was primarily on the systems side. I started to look at the bigger picture, got more questioning, viewed the overall situation as far as I could. I was moved into human resources for my computing expertise. I was expected from day one to know a reasonable amount of that. But over time, we're in a pretty good position in systems terms, because rather than looking at specific applications, I could say, but if we go this way, it gives us overall benefits rather than simply addressing individual needs. A third level course, Systems, Management, and Change, changed me the most.

What's been the impact of your studies on your career?

It was communication. I tended to be a loner, I liked to get on with things. But with tutorials, study groups, summer schools, you can't do that. While I don't consider myself a backroom boy who just wants to be left alone, it made me more ready to talk to people, to swap ideas, and not keep things closed in, because I notice that more in other people now, when they don't want to give you information. Either because of fear for their position, or wanting to be *the* knowledgeable person in a particular area. I'm quite happy to share information, and I'm better able to draw other people out now.

What's the most important use you make of your degree?

It will be useful if I actually have to look around at other careers. It gives me extra ammunition. I'm not desperately seeking to leave Marathon, but you see the way the economy's going, and the job market, and you keep one eye on the trade papers and see what jobs are going, and it quite often will say a degree is one of the requirements and you say, Well, that's a job I can now look for, whereas six years ago, I couldn't. With Marathon itself, the workforce has been shrinking. That reduces the number of opportunities to move around inside. So you do become a little bit unsettled.

What are your educational plans?

I'm about to start the Institute of Personnel Management which I am to do through the OU as well. Again, it's a career-related qualification specific to the personnel field. It will just broaden my horizons. It'll take three years at the most.

How has continuing your education changed your ideas about work?

It changed my idea of success. I realized that knowledge in itself was important to me, not as a means of getting to something else. I quite enjoyed meeting people who were happy with what they were doing. Getting to know other individuals, their backgrounds, likes and dislikes, gives you an ability to step back from yourself and say, Well, what I'm doing right now isn't bad. Some of my colleagues here see the career as *the thing* and certainly are more single-minded than I am.

My ideas about redundancy changed as well. Before I saw it as the end, a sudden full stop to a career. I see it now as a challenge, as a start. Partly because I am more confident and partly because the work I've done has given me a number of strengths. It was quite a dramatic change, this sudden realization of, 'Hang on, I'm looking at this the wrong way round.' The threat of redundancy is a big deal for a number of Marathon men, married, two or three young kids, not much chance of the wife going out and working, and they are the sole income.

I also feel differently about retirement, because I met a lot of retired people while doing the course, in tutorials and summer school who were having a whale of a time. In my twenties, anyone over forty didn't exist. And these people taught me there's a fair amount of life left at that stage. I can see myself doing various courses of choice. I may not wait until I retire. I've always wanted to do the Shakespeare third-level half-credit. I see myself studying more because I enjoy it than for another career, but I could get interested in a job in archaeology.

How did your studies affect your interests?

Greatly. Once I'd done the Arts foundation course, I was able to go to an art gallery and know a bit about various approaches to art, recognize the pictures that we'd studied, and talk about them with more understanding. I've been going to the National since, not for any specific exhibition, and right now I'm quite looking forward to the Faberge exhibit when it's in town.

And Julie and I have been going to the theatre more and the range of plays is much wider. Before I might have gone along occasionally to see a big West End musical, but now we go along to smaller theatres like the Almeida. We've gone there once every three months for the last couple of years. Right now I'm looking forward to seeing Richard Griffiths in *Galileo*.

In the course we also did Charles Dickens' *Hard Times*, which was quite an interesting exercise, and I enjoyed history very much because the approach was to the way historians get their primary sources. As a consequence I'm more interested in history and architecture. We went to Ephesus, a big ruined Roman city in Turkey last year, that they're still doing a hell of a lot of work on, and we'd like to see the terracotta warriors in China. In December we'll fly to Bali for five nights and then down to Australia, spend three weeks yachting, and then fly back via Hong Kong and see some of China. Then we're going to Thailand in October of 1995. I like to plan my holidays two or three years ahead.

Continuing my education got the ball rolling and the ball continues to roll. One of the reasons I want to go to Australia is because the couple we're going with, who live in Sydney, he has a skipper's license for a fairly large yacht and his wife has a license for a smaller type of craft. I don't have any yachting experience but I'm aiming to learn, because I think it would be quite a break from the routine. I'll start off doing dinghies down at the Welsh Reservoir off the North Circular Road. And then graduate to yachts before we go out to Australia, late summer. My wife wants to do this too, so it should be good fun.

Why would you recommend continuing education to other men?

Most people's attitude toward a degree is, a degree is a degree, however it's got. But you've also got people who say, Well, anyone who's done what you have is obviously quite determined. And others who say, I'm glad I went to university when I was young, because there is no way I could have done that, on my own. It gives you quite a good feeling when people say that.

I had a strange, anticlimactic feeling when I completed it, but suddenly people were saying, Well done, and sending cards, it gave it a finish. But the thing that really brings it home is the graduation ceremony. I'd said to my wife, I'm really not worried about going to the graduation ceremony. I've got the degree, it doesn't matter. And she said, No, no, you've done it and I'd like to come along and I'd like to see you in a robe and take some pictures. I said, Oh, all right then. I thoroughly enjoyed the whole day. It was at Wembley Conference Centre in June. It was organised really well, very dignified. When the Chancellor and all the rest were parading down, they played *Fanfare for A*

Common Man. It was quite moving and that brought home, I've done it. I and these other people, we're here for the same reason. Other men deserve that good feeling.

Why are men reluctant to take traditional women's jobs?

It's a status thing. Men see elementary teaching and nursing as not as high in status as an office person. You see men walking into a big office building like this. You don't actually know what they do in here, but the fact that they go in day in, day out, has more status than some bloke who teaches infants three afternoons a week. That's not the kind of thing you tell your friends over a few beers at the pub when everyone else is talking about manufacturing, money making, and office politics. To talk about the drawing that a seven-year-old produced that has real prospects for the future...it comes down to fear, fear of being looked down on, of being laughed at.

Why is it hard for many men to change?

Men today are insecure. Their position of *the* breadwinner was unchallenged for quite some time. Suddenly that isn't the case. It's still an attitude in men that they should be out, doing the work, and that is reflected in men's attitudes towards women in the work environment. They talk about this glass ceiling idea where a woman can get so far and no further. It's due to uncertainty and insecurity in men.

Women are much more adaptable, where a man will set out a career, or drift into a career, and then he has difficulty looking outside of that. My moving from the computing side into human resources was a fairly dramatic career change. A lot of men see *a* career and the steps in *that* career and find it difficult to move away from that. They're frightened of failing, frightened of regretting what they've done, of saying, Oh, I wish I'd stayed in the old career.

How does continuing education prepare men for change?

You realize that what you're doing is contributing overall to society. And that other people have also got their contributions to make. That applies to anybody from a managing executive to a cleaner. A cleaner is not a particularly high job status but if the cleaners weren't there, you'd soon know about it.

I find it depressing that the more jobless there are, the more threatened I feel. Earlier I talked about seeing redundancy as a chance, but that's me assuming that I'm going to be able to get something. As far as people who are out of work, I want to see them back in work. One, it makes me feel more secure, two, it benefits the economy, and three, it makes them feel that they're contributing to society. There is too much of a short-term view in Britain. Instead of planning ahead, there's always the need to satisfy the shareholders, make money as quickly as possible that benefits one small section of society greatly. But there are a hell of a lot of people who could be in useful work and because of the way the economic structure is now, they aren't allowed to. I found it depressing listening to the radio last night, talking to people in Cornwall where unemployment is particularly bad, asking, Are you able to to grasp the idea that you may never work again? And people said, Well, I don't want to, but I think I'm having to.

Imagine Marathon reorganized and there were no human resources jobs anywhere else. But you could get a job as a cleaner. Would you take it?

I would. I'd need to be occupied. And I'd say, while I'm doing this, in my free time, I can be looking for something else. Before doing the degree it was, this is what I do and I will be flexible only within the guidelines of this occupation. Somebody else did *that* work. But today, yes, I would be a cleaner.

———————————

Human resource specialists may well disappear in the next decade, replaced by the information highway. But there will always be cleaners.

Chapter 3

Job Dissatisfaction As the Norm

At the other end of the scale more and more people discover they are the new working poor.... Their paths out of this situation are closing down as the world in which they are trapped becomes meaner, harder and more corrupting. In between (the privileged class and the working poor) there are growing numbers of people who are insecure, fearful for their jobs in an age of permanent `down-sizing', `cost-cutting' and `casualisation' and ever more worried about their ability to maintain a decent standard of living (Hutton, p.3).

How happy in their work are the men you'll meet here? If I had to identify those least content, I'd have to say Tony (Chapter 18) who considers a gardener's job just a job. But the thing is, he gets along very well with his workmates now and that's new. And Mahmood (Chapter 12) who wishes that somehow his degree had led to a new occupation. He is, however, clearly contentedly reading, studying, and translating. So, given that dissatisfaction appears the norm throughout Great Britain, these men's overall sense of fulfillment from work is extraordinary.

Dissatisfaction throughout the land? Yes, only four in ten of the British workforce are happy in their work. Britain ranks number eight among eleven post-industrialised countries in job satisfaction. Brits feel insecure and stressed out, that they're not making enough money, their work isn't useful to society, *and* it exhausts them (McKie, 1993).

`There is no feel-good factor here. Job insecurity—that's the thing. That's the worst thing. It's what it's all about,' moans a fortysomething construction engineer. `Because even those who are left don't know where they are; and we're all monitoring each other. There's no training. I have to rob budgets to get professional training for my staff, for them not to fall behind. And there's people watching, and they're going to come in one day and sweep us away.' A younger insurance employee at a large company rife with redundancies, temporary contracts, and reliance on a 24-hour telephone line to deal with customers, seemed to take the feel-bad factor more in his stride. `The culture of work is changing, and we can see the way it's going, but some people can't change. First thing you notice, they're having an outburst in the office. Just shouting. Everything begins to fall apart (Parker, 1994).'

The men in charge of downsizing and job-redefining aren't any happier. A 1994 *Observer*/Gallup survey of managers (profile: male 35 or over, married, well paid, highly educated) reported their workloads were increased, jobs less secure, home life suffering, promotions not forthcoming, and staff development, *their special thing*, eliminated by cost-cutting (Caulkin, 1994). Likewise, an Institute of Management survey of 1,100 managers found record levels of stress due to increased workloads, longer hours, unreasonable deadlines, and unpaid overtime. Two-thirds of the managers said their professional and personal lives were unsynchronised; there was no time for partners or hobbies (Tooher, 1996).

Dissatisfaction is bad for your health and your family

British workers are so stressed out they take twice as much sick leave as the Germans. A British worker takes 7.4 days off sick each year compared to 3.7 for a German worker. The cost to the economy due to illness was £15 billon a year, but the cost in human suffering and premature death, well, how do we measure that (Leathley, 1994)?

Fear of redundancy means that a quarter of all British male employees work more than the 48 hours a week. The European Union would like to set 48 hours as an absolute maximum. A Demos survey found that people are more bothered about time, that is, the lack of it for family and friends, than they have been for years. 'I've no social life; I'm too knackered. I work and then it's to bed. That's all.' 'I know other people who have got to where I want to be but their personal lives are a nightmare.' 'I see my boyfriend for about an hour a day. It would be nice to eat together' (Mulgan & Wilkinson, 1995).

A classic case of dissatisfaction

About one hundred of 800 staff at Britain's most famous publishing house, Penguin UK, were let go before Christmas 1995. A bestselling author described the total disarray. 'It's a terrible place at the moment, very unhappy. Quite a few authors feel adrift there. I'm seriously thinking of going elsewhere.' The employees left behind felt undervalued, undermined and completely demoralised. They were terrified of more sackings and suffering unacceptable levels of stress trying to cope with huge workloads. The old guidelines about promotion were gone and no one knew who it was important to impress anymore (Lord, 1996).

Lawry Rhodes of Chapter 4 is another classic case. His building society employer forced him to entice customers to buy policies that were unsuitable for them and if he didn't meet company goals, he was harangued throughout his half-hour annual interview with senior management. The job became so morally repugnant that, after sixteen years, Lawry quit. And you might not think work in a packing factory would be satisfying, but in comparison, it was. Note also Lawry's comments on what parents' overwork is doing to children.

Chapter 4

Lawry Rhodes, Who Took His Time

When it started, the sun swept up the black dust swastika
and swirled the planets— concentrated the light and the darkness.

And the light shook each ripple of evolution as far as the comets—
white brine and flotsam off the wave washed back to time.

We've maybe one chance to see this chalk-stick smudge obliterate its own geometry,
the perihelion passage across our sky.

Each capture and escape is the pencil line before and after
always forming the petal around the fire.

This poem, `The fire and the rose', by Lawry Rhodes appeared in the journal *Iron*, Edition 54, 1988. It's related to one of the rarer outcomes of continuing education, a complete career change—from building society manager to English teacher.

Lawry met me at the door of Bexhill High School looking every bit the teacher he had been for the past four months—brown tweed jacket, tan trousers, trim beard, big smile. He had just turned 42. Born into a large working class family in Bramley, Leeds, he earned twelve O-levels and three A-levels. His father was a policeman, his mother worked for the Inland Revenue. After Lawry failed his second year law exams at Nottingham University, he became a building society manager. He moved to Bexhill ten years ago. He is married with one daughter, age fourteen. He started studying with the OU in 1981 and got his BA in 1993.

Your reasons for doing a university degree?

I wanted to put right having failed the first time round. Because we've always been competitive educationally. Coming from a large family, from a not so well off background, we kids felt under pressure to achieve so I didn't take the idea of not succeeding at something for granted.

But I also wanted to do a subject that I enjoyed doing, something for pleasure, and see where it led me. I started with the Arts Foundation course. What appealed to me was that it was interdisciplinary, music, poetry, theatre, history and philosophy. It gave me insight into so many things I had forgotten since leaving school. I suddenly found that I could understand poetry, particularly modern poetry.

My motives changed half way through when I decided to change careers. I reassessed my situation and used a more conscious approach to each subject to insure that I got the right qualification for teaching. For teaching, in secondary school in particular, you have to have a specialised degree, it can't be interdisciplinary. That advice came over very clearly from the OU at the right time in 1989 when I spoke to a number of people at the regional centre. Their advice was you've got to put all your eggs into one basket and make it look good. So I had to postpone doing my studies until the right courses came up because I'd run out of literature courses to do. I'd done poetry, Shakespeare, the romantic poets course. I was in Eastbourne library one day, having broken my studies for a year or two, and discovered the university was proposing to do a couple of new courses in literature, Literature in the Modern World and a 4th-level course on post-colonial literature. So it took me from 1981 to 1993 with numerous gaps.

What obstacles did you have?

My employers' anti-intellectual attitude was my only real obstacle. At best they were indifferent, and at other times they were downright hostile. Certain people in middle-management without any formal qualifications, in the generation before me, were in fear of underlings with qualifications. Every time I mentioned the possibility of getting financial support, it was always negative. But it wasn't the lack of financial support that bothered me. They could have said we're pleased that you're doing it, we recognize the fact that it will enhance your involvement in life and your job and may even benefit the organisation. But they never said it once. They made me almost lead a double life. I wasn't to let people know that I was doing a degree because the standard response was, `Oh, he might be good at doing exams, he might be good on paper, but can he do the job?'

How have your studies changed you?

I was able to work out my feelings about my earlier life, which you tend to do in the middle part of your life, through poetry. For five years, between '83 and '88, I wrote. What really helped me develop in writing was the OU Poets, a workshop magazine, a completely self-generating group of writers. You'd send some poetry in to an editor, by rotation, a different editor each month, and you'd comment on other people's poems from the previous time. It was a fairly friendly environment and from that I learned you could not only write for an audience and learn how your poems are received, you could publish in a professional magazine.

My studies also gave me the self-confidence to get seriously involved in local theatre. Because I want to do what I want to do and say what I want to say. It made me feel more confident about public speaking, I became less withdrawn, it even affected my posture. People used to say I always had my head down.

What else about your previous career made you want to change?

The way the financial markets were collapsing, the more the society put pressure on the staff to, first of all, sell things. There was pressure to virtually blackmail people. You were giving someone, say, a mortgage interview where their potential home is at stake, and subtly leading them toward policies and financial products which were not suitable for them at all. In order that the society would benefit financially. The profit motive was taking over the principle of mutuality in building societies. These pressures were consistently applied over six years from 1987 to 1993; we were constantly required to account for why we hadn't sold products of a certain type, and it's not surprising now that many of these organisations are receiving civil actions and prosecutions and investigations into the way these products were sold. I felt morally disgruntled about it and I felt I had no contact with my organisation. They gave me a half-hour interview a year with a senior manager and it was all statistics and nothing positive on what you'd achieved, it was about what you hadn't achieved and what you must do and if you don't, this will happen. So I resigned.

But my resignation also had to do with the summer of 1992 when I needed to study to capacity to get a good grade, a 1, to get into teaching. I needed to prove my degree was up-to-date because I would be starting at forty. The older you are and the more job experience you have, the more the local authority might have to pay you. Those sixteen years with the building society made me quite expensive to employ. So I'm very grateful to my present employer!

How has continuing your education changed your ideas about work?

I had thoughts of becoming a teacher when I was in secondary school but I didn't want to spend the whole of my life in the classroom. I think everything's worked out for the best, coming in as a mature student. You can't teach at the level you should be doing for a whole lifetime, and enjoy it and be effective. I don't expect to be teaching for the whole of my life in a secondary school like this one. I would like to experience different kinds of teaching. I want to be successful in each particular job and give it the right amount of time, if I can do that.

How did your studies affect your interests, apart from poetry?

It changed my interests towards all the arts. When I worked for the building society, I was expected to join organisations like the Junior Chamber of Commerce. It was more like the boys club with the undercurrent of chatting each other up for business. They forced you into professional circles, bankers, soliciters, accountants, so they'd invest money in your building society. You were all pally with them, played golf. I never spent my expense account because I didn't enjoy those business lunches. I'm not a guy's guy, I'm not really interested in football, rugby, motor racing, the manly things supposedly. I think men have got to change anyway and become more adaptable, flexible, and able to talk about a wider range of things. The ordinary Italian or Spanish male is much more cultured than a middle-manager in England. For that reason I tend to enjoy conversations more with women than men.

What was most important in your life before and after the degree?

Before going back to studying, it was survival in economic terms. Being responsible for a young child, you have to toe the line. Whatever conformity the organisation you're in requires is important. Now, after, what's most important is enjoying whatever I'm doing. Now it's being able to be interested in the arts.

It got started with the kind of knock-about things that you put on at the end of summer school, a review. We had been studying *A Midsummer Night's Dream* so we did a scene from it. It was the first time I've ever done any acting. We got quite a lot of laughs from that. Then I auditioned for a part in a local amateur theatre group production in *The Rivals* by Sheridan, and even though it was only a laughable church hall production, I thought we achieved quite a good standard. I've tried to do as much acting as possible since, without it taking over my life. I've got a rehearsal tonight. A cast of four. I'm directing *Relatively*

Speaking by Alan Ayckbourn. BATS, the Bexhill Amateur Theatrical Society, decided to put this play on and were searching for a director so I volunteered. I prefer to act. I love the open-air Shakespeare in Manor Gardens in Bexhill, early August. A wonderful setting. My daughter takes part, so she's an actress as well now.

And for my school I'm writing an adaptation of HG Wells' *War of the Worlds*. As a musical. I've already written three scenes. If you get a chance, listen to Jeff Wayne's music for *War of the Worlds* with Richard Burton narrating. It's not written for the stage, but the music is excellent and we have an ex-pupil, a professional musician, who's thinking of bringing all these synthesizers down. And we've got a supply teacher whose husband is brilliant at lighting and he's hoping to create these special effects of the Martian tripods. It would be a play with dance and rock music with the kids playing drums and guitars, but we're having to make up a whole story line to fill the gaps in the music.

Why would you recommend continuing education to other men?

Because you're given support to change. I was cooped up where I was, I was being contained by my organisation and by my own conformity and while I didn't have any health problems because of my job, it felt like a midlife bursting through, that I had to do something different. My tutors played a role in that change and supported me. When I resigned from the company, I did feel very exposed, like I was cutting myself off from my bread and butter, that it was a dangerous thing to do.

To succeed, however, you've got to have a very strong interest in the subject. You can't fight the competition from other pressures in your life if you're not really interested in what you're learning. Because you're not sharing the experience of learning in a classroom with other students. You're constantly in an isolated situation. At the end of the day, it is about doing TMAs and reading background material on your own. Another thing, there is a lot to be said for taking the long run. If I had rushed my degree through, I would have come out with a 2.2, a 2.1 at the most. Instead, by taking my time and enjoying what I've done, I got first class honours and at midlife, because of that, I have the opportunity to progress in teaching.

Why is it hard for the average man to change careers?

Frankly, I couldn't recommend doing what I did because I had no job to go to. I left my job because my grades were suffering from the pressures at work and I couldn't let that happen. I had just come back from summer school. I was going into teaching. It felt right. Then to go back to that awful job, it all felt wrong. In that emotional state, because of my age, coming up to forty, I had to make the break, fly blind, take what came. If anybody else is prepared to take that chance, with a big mortgage hanging over his head, and the risks and stresses involved, if he has enough confidence in himself, he can do it.

I got jobs. I got work for six weeks in a packing factory. It was great. £3.50 an hour, getting up at four o'clock in the morning. Wonderful. But no real worries. I could sit in the canteen and read my post-colonial literature and nobody bothered me and there was no baggage to carry home with me at the end of the day.

Continued study is the answer for men who have to go through different jobs, which is now the case. You don't have a job for life. You may have to be a roadsweeper one year, a packer in a pharmaceutical factory the next, and then a civil servant after the factory job. You need all the literacy skills and social skills, skills of interaction, you can get. Men taught the sport mentality, the kick'em and run approach, team-building through aggression, have got to learn to behave differently in today's complex work environments.

What's the biggest challenge in teaching today?

There are pockets around here of quite substantial deprivation. It's an area heavily dependent on self-employment. People here have a buccaneering attitude, an independent feeling that they can make it on their own. The recession knocked that out of people in the building trade in the Southeast. A lot of people have lost jobs and for those who still have them, there's not enough time for parents to devote to their children. There's a lot of emotional deprivation here. These children are not getting enough attention at home so they fight with each other for attention at school, whether positively by doing well, or negatively by misbehaving.

Moving out to these rural estates has not improved the quality of interaction among people. Children lack contact with a wider family network, where they could also get attention from cousins, aunties, uncles, grandparents. From that old working class street life and community. Another major problem is role models for boys. In an age when warfare should be being stopped, we should be moving away from role models like Sylvester Stallone and Arnold Schwartzenegger and the heavy guy image. So the challenge for teachers is to find a substitute.

––––––––––––

I don't know which is more to be admired, Lawry's new career in teaching or his new avocation as an actor. Rifkin and Handy might say it's his involvement with the cultural life of his community because community is where the solution to the global unemployment mess has to be found.

Chapter 5

Stress of Presenteeism

Mr Wasilewski joined his present company, a fund management company, in April 1994, to be responsible for a 21-strong UK Equity team. On average he works about 60 hours a week, generally between 8 am and 8 pm, but sometimes longer. "When the dinners and client meetings in the evenings kick in I don't get home until 10.30 or 11 pm. If there is a special project on, the hours are just silly. I can work 14 hours a day, seven days a week for the best part of six weeks." Since Gabriella arrived, Mr Wasilewski has tried to get home earlier. "Gabriella doesn't go to bed early so I get to see her in the evenings. Sometimes if I've had a hard day I'm exhausted but Gabriella is a joy of a baby, a form of relaxation and such a change from work (Garner, 1995)."

Mr. Wasilewski's got a new disease, presenteeism. That's being at work when you shouldn't be because (a) you're too worn out to be effective, or (b) there isn't any work to do, or (c) both of the above, which is really silly. Presenteeism dates back to 1981 when Thatcherism gave birth to yuppies and work became the status symbol that leisure had been. People boasted about working 12- and 13-hour days, how they only saw their partners for an hour now and again, how they had no time to read books or discuss ideas with friends, and how they hadn't had a holiday for simply years.

Presenteeism is the price paid by the people who get left behind after the big layoffs because now they must put in longer hours to make up for the work their former colleagues did. And, naturally, the still-employed are anxious to show the organisation that they're committed, in case there's a second round of redundancies. Which there will be. People suffering from chronic overemployment haven't even got time to spend the income that's still coming in.

That alarming equation again

A young friend with a new job in a London bank refuses to have a drink with Charles Handy in *The Empty Raincoat* (1995b). The guy said he couldn't get away until nine pm because his group expected him to work that late, and Saturdays too, and while the work was exhilarating and well paid, it totally consumed him. His irritated partner, not surprisingly, thought the bank was nuts and asked, 'Why don't they employ twice as many people at half the salary and work them half as hard? That way they could all lead a normal life.'

Ah, but that wouldn't make good corporate sense, would it? The bank has gone the other way, the formula introduced in Chapter 1: $1/2 \times 2 \times 3 = P$. P as in Profit. For the bank. No wonder 'The British work the longest average week in the European Union. Sixteen per cent of the British work more than 48 hours a week—twice as many people as in any other European country. We have fewer public holidays than any other EU country. We seem to be heading inexorably towards the work-orientated society that exists in the United States where the average employee works 164 hours more per year than 20 years ago (O'Kelly, 1994).'

Jobs hardest hit

The most stressful jobs in the 1990s are those where truly radical change and restructuring are taking place. They are:

Teachers—heads must manage their own budgets and there have been widespread moves towards assessing teachers and performance-related pay. Every other week some newspaper claims 5,000 or 10,000 or 15,000 need to be fired because they're incompetent.

Doctors, dentists and nurses—restructuring means the docs must manage their own budgets; low nurses' wages discourage new entrants.

Social workers—under-funded and under-resourced with impossible workloads dealing with ever more difficult people.

Police, fire officers, ambulance service—restructuring means job cuts and lost lives.

Middle managers—being pruned to a running-scared core elite.

Blue collar workers—long, unhealthy, unsafe hours in construction and mining for those still in work.

Public utility workers—privatisation means having to say 'Goodbye. Sorry,' when it comes to jobs.

Media workers—jobs are out, contracts in.

Allegedly, litigation is in the pipeline to relieve the impossible hours of junior hospital doctors and the massive workloads of senior social workers (Boseley, 1994).

The sex hardest hit

The 'long hours culture' is harder on men than women. Among office staff, men work longer hours than women, with 81 per cent saying they work forty hours or more weekly compared to 56 per cent of women. Thirty-seven per cent of men work fifty hours or more compared with thirteen per cent of women. One reason for the difference is the higher level of men's work: 45 per cent of male senior white-collar staff work 50 hours or more a week. And more men than women complain that their work performance suffers as hours grow longer. Surprisingly, 90 per cent of employers admit the long hours culture reduces performance and lowers morale (Moyes, 1995). But don't expect them to do anything about it.

How stress hits

Quoting from an article titled `Stress, panic and you'—`My palms started sweating, and I couldn't see clearly. I felt as if I was going to faint, but I didn't, and the feeling of slipping away stayed with me. Travelling home on the Tube I was very afraid, and the world suddenly seemed like a terrifying place. When I got home I was too nervous to eat. I tried to watch the television but I couldn't find a programme that didn't make me feel frightened. All the time I had this sharp pain at the bottom of my back and in the centre of my head at the back, where I'd never had pains before. I went to bed and lay there shaking. I was convinced I was losing my mind.'

Three out of four people may be experiencing too much stress in the workplace. Worst affected are single professionals between 25 and 35. Your whole body gets involved in a panic attack like the one described above, the entire hormonal system, cardiovascular system, immune system. But when people feel powerless to improve their job situation, about the only thing they can think of is to show up, regardless.

Forty per cent of absenteeism from work is thought to be stress-related, that's 40 per cent of 25 billion working days a year. But the loss in productivity due to the stress of presenteeism is anybody's guess. Ravi Shankar's music is supposed to help. German researchers have found that of all the different music played in an experiment, the only sound that reduced listeners' blood pressure and stress hormones was Ravi's (Watson, 1996).

I didn't know about the Shankar technique when I interviewed Lamber Dosanjh of Chapter 6, but what he spontaneously told me was that long ago, to keep his stress level low, he made the positive decision he would never accept promotion to management.

Chapter 6

Lamber Dosanjh, Who Said No to Managing

Worrying doesn't help. I have done the best I can for the company. I trained myself at my expense. And got ready for the changes they expect us to handle. I didn't sit back saying, the company owes me a living, or somebody else does. I've gone out and prepared myself to face any change that comes my way. If that's not good enough, that's life, somebody has to go. Say, I'm fifty-five and somebody's thirty-five, obviously, I don't mind if I have to go instead of him. He's got his whole work life ahead and I'm happy in what I've achieved.

Camelford House is a big bland block of a building on windy Albert Embankment. Lots of security officials about, questions to answer, visitors books to sign, ID cards to be worn about the neck. Plump, bespectacled, black-haired Lamber, in contrast, was a picture of relaxed informality in his short-sleeved print shirt and gray trousers as he led me to a conference room for our interview.

Lamber is 51, began studying with the OU in 1988, and got his BSc in 1995. He has been with British Telecom for 25 years, a technical officer for twenty years. His wife works at Heathrow in customs, and they have a grown daughter who studied German and European studies, and a grown son who is into business information. Lamber has the equivalent of six O-levels. A Sikh, he was born in Jullunder, India and came to the UK in 1962 by way of Tanzania. His mother and father joined him in 1964 but, sadly, his father died the next year, prematurely.

Your reasons for doing a university degree?

I always wanted a degree and I thought this was a good way to do it. But my main reason was our jobs were changing a lot. We were shifting to computerized communications. I wanted to learn about computers. I always watched educational programs on telly anyway because I was interested in many of them. I delayed starting for several years, but once I decided, then I had no real problems, even though I took both the maths and science foundation courses in the first year. I got a phone call from the OU saying, Are you sure you can manage 16 TMAs and 16 CMAs, 32 in all? I did have difficulty keeping track of them. It was a lot of work because I hadn't studied for twenty-seven years.

What obstacles did you have?

My early obstacle to education was financial. My parents couldn't afford to send me to university. I always knew I could have done it, but we didn't have the money. I started with science and math because they'd be the easiest courses to do. I couldn't have done the arts foundation course because I had no background in the arts.

Obviously, I spent so much time studying, I had less time to get together with my friends and relations. It was a problem because my friends were reluctant to disturb me. They knew I was working hard and studying hard, so it did cut down on my social life. Now that I have finished, it's not that easy to suddenly start socialising again. It will take time.

How have your studies changed you?

The first courses made the biggest difference. I became disciplined because I had to be. I learned how to make use of my time. I had to set deadlines for the assignments. Prioritize. I now manage my time much more effectively at work. Before I wasn't conscious of time. Once you realize there is a limited amount of it, you make better use of it.

Also, it has made me feel successful. I wanted to achieve this degree at this time of my life. I didn't want promotion to management or anything like that. This was what I wanted and I got it and I'm happy. Another man might decide he wants to get into higher management, but then not get promoted as high as he would like. He may feel he didn't achieve what he wanted and that somehow he's a failure. I've succeeded because I achieved exactly what I set out to achieve.

What's been the impact of your studies on your career?

My job changes virtually every year. Without my studies I would have struggled. I had colleagues who were afraid to move to the new technology and they said they didn't want to be re-trained, so they left. They thought they wouldn't like office-type work. The biggest switch for me was in 1990. Before 1990 I used to work in the exchange which was electromechanical and then suddenly my job became an office-based job working on the computers. If I hadn't done the courses, I couldn't have coped. Even so, it took me a year to settle into the office routine which is completely different from engineering work in the exchange.

Keeping up my education made it easier to deal with the process of BT's laying people off which has been going on for the last five years. They have a target of 15,000 jobs a year. For the rest of us, we have to continually learn new jobs. It helps if you have a qualification. And in the process of doing the courses, you learn how to teach yourself. So if you have to learn some new software on your latest job, you can pick it up. I can read the books and do whatever needs to be done to adapt.

I decided very soon after I joined the company never to be a manager. That's one reason I didn't do the course earlier. Because the company might have looked at that qualification and asked if I wished to be promoted. And I would have had to turn them down.

What's the most important use you make of your degree?

Under normal circumstances I would have got a promotion, to a higher grade at least, but with BT losing jobs, with the cutbacks, that's not possible. I only got my final results around Christmas so I'm still getting used to the idea that I have this new qualification. I'll start thinking now, what use can I make of it and we'll see how it goes. The funny thing is, I don't feel any different. Maybe after the ceremony it will sink in. Right now it just feels like there's a gap in my life.

I get a lot of satisfaction from having done it. When I started the course I wasn't sure I could keep up. BT paid the expenses for the first two years, but then they said we don't really need you to be trained for this job, it's not going to help us. So I paid the expenses after that. I wanted to do it for myself. It does impress the company, supposedly, but so far they haven't acted on it.

Frankly, I never talk about what I've done, my BSc, in the office. I only mention it to people who are close to me. It's something I did for its own sake. My boss has to know, so he can take it into account, but the rest of the people don't have to know about it.

What are your educational plans?

I've always wanted to learn another language. So I'm thinking about which one to learn. German, French, Spanish, Italian. I'm also interested in learning more about gardening and plants. I've always wanted to grow unusual plants. I'm looking forward to gardening now that I have some spare time. I can spend more time in Kew Gardens too, it's very peaceful, you can forget you are in the middle of London, can't you?

How has continuing your education changed your ideas about work?

With technological advances we're supposed to have shorter working hours and more leisure time, which isn't happening. They're using smaller numbers of people to do the work. Eventually society will have to face it and rather than working a forty-hour week, we should work a 30-hour week and employ more people. We can't keep having so many people not doing anything. It's such a waste, especially school leavers with no prospect of having a job. If I have to retire early, tomorrow or next year, I've been lucky.

This country has changed a lot since the 80s. We were made to say, you look after yourself, and people became more selfish. This is what has happened in big companies. The executives give themselves huge pay rises. How can one person deserve a £100,000 pay rise? The wrong people are getting rewarded. And the people who are really doing the work get laid off. It doesn't give the average employee much incentive. I would rather have 1% rise if everybody got the same.

What was most important in your life before and after the degree?

Before I started studying, I simply wanted my children to succeed. Most important was to get their education right, I wasn't that high a priority. I did get excited when I started in 1988, but most of all, I wanted them to be educated.

Now what I most look forward to is to have good health and a happy retirement. I'll be 52 in October, so at most I have eight years to go. I'm planning to retire at sixty, but earlier would be all right. When I decide which language I'm going to learn, then we'll travel to that country. If you want to travel abroad, knowing the language makes it more enjoyable wherever you go. My wife and I definitely will travel when the children are settled down. Right now they are still living with us.

The trouble with most parents is, you tend to do the opposite of what was done to you. If your parents were strict, you tend to relax a bit. Or if they had been lax, you tend to be strict. You say, I wish my parents had treated me this way, and then you do it that way. I was raised for my first thirteen years by my grandmother, in India. I only saw my parents every five years because they had moved to East Africa. Because I missed my parents so much, I'm spoiling my children. My parents probably didn't realize how much effect being apart from them would have on me. You should be with your parents at a young age. The thing is, I was in India, then I went to East Africa for two years, and then came here to be with my brother. So I had a very short time with my father and you've got to be with a person to know him.

That's why I spend time with my children, no matter what. And when it comes to jobs around the house, we're leaving them alone. My wife and I share the household chores. There's no one job which only one of us will do. Especially if my wife's on shift work and comes home late, I do the cooking.

Why would you recommend continuing education to other men?

I wanted to be better at my job and my changing work pattern was my main reason. It helps a man's self-confidence at work. If you don't continue with your education, all people have to judge you by is your day-to-day performance. This way, you have proved something else to them. When you get a qualification, people say, Oh, yes, he's done that. It was very hard to study so intensively that first year and I'm glad I didn't find out in advance how much work was involved. But those first courses gave me the confidence to do the later ones because every course I did was new material. There was nothing I had done before. There is no better preparation for a job that is constantly shifting.

But if you want to broaden your mind, or be a better person, you should do non-science subjects. The closest I came was DT200, how information technology is affecting people. The social implications of technology was for me a totally different way of thinking. For example, in banking, you can draw your money out whenever you want now, use credit cards, but these things are only helpful to people who've got bank accounts. The same with the information highway. If you don't own a computer, it might as well not exist. A lot of people still don't have access to this new information technology. I had never thought before about who benefits, that it all depends where you stand socially. For me, learning a new language will be part of that other process of broadening yourself.

It is a very good experience to meet people from other walks of life. I had worked with the same company for so long I was always dealing with the same people. I'm still in touch with other students I met on the foundation courses. My best friend is younger than I am and on some of the computing courses, he was helpful to me. We just got on. He's a shop manager with one of the big supermarkets, but he had the same interest I did, computers, and wanted to make more use of them, like I did. He's from Scotland. We've been in touch for seven years now. Even to find one friend is to gain a lot.

When Lamber finally leaves BT and his workplace colleagues for good, he'll still have the old buddies he met in tutorials and at summer school, plus new buddies he'll meet in further education classes. For any man who feels he didn't see enough of his father, what better way to really get to know other men than by learning something new together?

Chapter 7

Stress of Obsolescence

For two decades unemployment has been a grim fact of British life, bearing particularly hard on men. As well as those included in the official count who want work and can't find it, there are millions more who are marginalised—prematurely retired or living off inadequate savings or sickness benefit. One in four of the country's males of working age is now either officially unemployed or idle, with incalculable consequences for our well-being and social cohesion (Hutton, p.1).

Imagine a country where the unemployment rate is just five per cent, new jobs are growing rapidly and prospects are excellent. If you are a woman in Britain, you are in that picture. Now compare that scenario with a country where unemployment is more than thirteen per cent, where jobs are disappearing and the outlook is grim. If you are a man in Britain, this is your country. By the year 2000, women will account for nearly half the jobs in Britain. The female labour force is going to grow by 500,000 while the male labour force drops 300,000. Already 16-19 year-old girls have more jobs than 16-19 year-old boys.

Gone forever is the idea that the male full-time worker is the backbone of the workforce. In 1990, there were more than 11 million men working full-time. In 1993 the figure was 9.6 million and falling. Rising, however, were government benefit payments—wives' part-time jobs aren't enough to support a family (David Smith, 1994).

`It is mainly men who are the cause of the problem. Not only are there 1.7 million officially unemployed and dependent upon income support—there are another 2 million who are no longer even seeking employment because they know there is none. With each unemployed or non-employed man costing £9,000 a year in lost tax and income support, the transformation in the male labour market is costing the Exchequer over £36 billion a year (Hutton, p.185).'

The spectre of unemployment

That spectre is 34-year-old Mick who hasn't worked in twelve years and who spends his days lying in bed or staring at the back of his mother's head as she watches television. He is six stone overweight and his concentration is shot.

Both he and his mum despise him because he is a sponger and a slob and both have given up on the idea he'll ever do anything with his life. His major preoccupations are washing his socks and stroking the cat. Many years ago he was a clerical officer with the Inland Revenue. Then he decided to quit and study fine art. But he couldn't get a grant, so it was back to job-hunting, except now there were no jobs. And `over the years I've been totally cleansed of the work ethic. There are 5 billion people on the planet, so why should I do anything? Is it really necessary? (Weir, 1994)'

Obsolescence can lead to...

Obesity, if your Mum, like Mick's, is still prepared to feed you. Alcoholism, if you can pick up the wherewithal in spare change. Divorce. Every other marriage in Britain in 1996 was doomed to end in divorce, by far the worst record in the EU and one of the worst in the world. Experts say it's partly because the UK has one of the highest ratios of full-time working women, and that ever more British women are going out to work and becoming independent. Men are angry being out of work, or even if they're in work, they resent not being *the* breadwinner. Women, in turn, resent men's resentment and find it easier to raise their children without husbands, so that's what's happening (Delgado, 1996).

Obsolescence also leads to unmarriageability in the first place. Take Barry Percival, age 23, living with his parents, laid off from a production line job in a paving-stone factory a year ago. Now, a year out of work, his dole has been cut and he gets £36 income support a week. He says, `I don't think about girlfriends at the moment. I wouldn't even consider going out with a girl, let alone get married while I'm unemployed. I want to be like my dad, who went out to work every day and brought the money home to feed me and my sister while my mother stayed at home. I mean, it's a man's job to go out and work isn't it? You'd feel stupid sitting at home all day long with nothing to do. And I would hate it if she got a part-time job and I couldn't get work. As a man I find it very frightening that there are no full-time jobs to go to. For me, part-time work isn't worth going for financially.'

Barry doesn't think he'll ever make enough money to support a family. And he believes that women would rather live on the state than marry men who cannot support them (Driscoll, 1994).

The waste of younger men

Life expectancy for those at the bottom of the income scale has actually fallen. A sense that things are never going to get better lowers the will to live. On the

Continent, where incomes are distributed more evenly, life expectancy is two years longer than in Britain.

Low self-esteem is stressful and makes people more vulnerable to illness and death before their time. As income disparity has grown here, the group hardest hit is men aged 15 to 24. Their relative earnings have deteriorated, their unemployment rate has shot up, and their benefit entitlement has gone down. They have responded with a sharp rise in suicide rate (Hutton, 1996).

The waste of older men

If you are on an aeroplane when something goes very wrong, would you rather have a 50-year-old pilot or a 25-year-old pilot? Right. When I board a plane I like to see some gray hair in that cockpit.

But one in four men over age 55, and half of men over 60, are no longer in work. Thirty years ago, more than 95 per cent of those aged 55-59 and more than 90 per cent of those between 60-64 were still in work. A quarter worked on past 65. Now, fewer than one in ten does. Organisations are losing valuable experience and commitment. And the pensioned over-55s are losing, not only money, but stimulation, friends, a sense of contributing to society. During the economic boom of the late 1980s, droves of over-55s eagerly returned to the workforce, not necessarily full-time or doing heavy work, but clearly demonstrating that they wanted jobs (Timmins, 1996b).

Why a job at that age?

Will Hutton again. 'Even for those whose wages and conditions are poor...the rhythm of work gives life meaning. The achievement of new tasks, the acquisition of skills and the social intercourse that is part and parcel of the work experience is not something human beings want to avoid; they want and need it. Above all, work offers a sense of place in a hierarchy of social relations, both within the organisation and beyond it, and men and women are, after all, social beings. Inevitably some work is demeaning and poorly paid, but the same need is there. Those who work belong; those who do not are excluded (p.100).'

Steven Barker in the next chapter understands the need to work perhaps best of all of the men. Once his factory folded, the only jobs available to him were no skills jobs. He took them, nonetheless, because they allowed him time and energy to study and to become qualified. Now a social worker, he works with clients who have never held a job and he asks, How do you understand someone who has *never* had that need met?

Chapter 8

Steven Barker, Ratcatcher Who Made the Grade

I've never liked the underdog being dealt a bad deal, and sometimes I saw myself as the underdog, particularly when I was made redundant and the difficulty I had trying to get a job. It wasn't until I had some courses under my belt, that people started taking me seriously. Studying early on, I felt if somebody'd give me a chance, I could prove myself, but nobody was prepared to. It's only by continuing your education that you can find any way out. It's a hard way, but it is a way out.

Steven Barker has sparkling brown eyes, long brown hair, and wears an earring in his left ear. He was born in 1955 into a working-class family, left North Romford Comprehensive with no O-levels, and worked from 1974 to 1983 as an automotive paint technician. Made redundant, he began his OU studies which finished with an honours BA in 1993. He is now a qualified social worker employed in long-term child care for Essex Social Services. He is currently working on a MSc in counselling psychology at the University of East London. His wife works in local government in the housing department. We did the interview at his dining table surrounded by his nine-year-old daughter's Barbie dolls, a wall of framed family photos, and four cats taking morning naps.

Your reasons for doing a university degree?

Redundancy from the paint industry after ten years. When I left school, at 16, I went into the City to work in the civil service. It was considered a job for life. My parents come from a background of the Depression when there was no work, and if you had a job, then you were fine. So they encouraged me to stick to that. It was possible then to walk out of your job on a Friday and have a good job on the Monday. And each time I changed there would be a progression in wages. But I never felt that working in an office really fulfilled my idea of what I should be doing, so I did a City and Guilds qualification in laboratory science. My father supported me for a year and then I went to work in the paint industry. They gave me a further apprenticeship and I progressed to a supervisory role.

But the competition was too great from abroad. There was a lot of rationalisation in the industry and in 1983 a lot of redundncies. I was one of them. I couldn't do anything else and I was approaching the great age of thirty. I was in a quite frightening position and I applied for any job available. We're talking about the market of no skills jobs. I also went to work voluntarily at the Citizens Advice Bureau because I didn't want to be at home doing nothing. I wanted to be able to say to prospective employers, I am occupied.

I had enjoyed interacting with people in my union, so I thought the CAB would give me some skills I was looking for. When I was there I met the head of children's homes for the local authority, and she said, I understand that you're looking for work. I can offer you three months employment. It was around Christmas time but I had never worked with children. I took it but I was terrified. I'd had no experience with children other than my cousins.

That job stretched into eighteen months. But like all poorly paid jobs, there was no career structure. It was a deadend occupation and `you pay peanuts and you get monkeys doing the job.' It wasn't for me, but I felt the direction I was moving in and I knew I needed to re-educate myself. I chose the OU because I had to go for it in a big way and fail, rather than prolong the agony.

I took an unskilled job which gave me hours that allowed me to study. I worked for the environmental health department as a drainman and a pest control officer. We did the really nasty jobs, nine to five. I used to pick up incontinent waste. We had to clear out houses where people had died or left them in a terrible state. Rats everywhere. But, I was able to study in the evening and at lunch in the library.

What obstacles did you have?

I was lucky to have had an extremely good tutor on my first course, social science foundation, because if I hadn't had her support, I might not have got through the course and that would have been it. I had attempted in the past to do O-levels and it had come to nothing, so I had very little confidence in myself. I didn't tell my parents straight away. I wanted to pass the first year first.

Then because I was becoming more financially secure, we thought we should start a family, because we'd been married eight years. At the same time I became a bit overambitious. I took several courses. With the birth of my daughter, it became too disruptive and I failed that year. I wasn't put off by it. I thought, I've tried to run before I can walk. Wasted my time. So I took each course in its turn.

The men I worked with weren't interested in that sort of thing, getting on, bettering themselves. They would see that as getting above your station. I had to hide what I was doing, not to be ridiculed. If they knew I was studying for a degree, they would have said, Why would you want to do that?

But that was nothing compared to the women students I met. A lot had partners who were very threatened by it. They had to deal with violence, marriage breakups, being a single parent. I was whinging about the people I worked with when I met a woman at summer school who was a dinner lady in her fifties. She was going to graduate the following year. And she hadn't told her family in all those years, because of ridicule. She'd studied for the whole of her degree after school. The school provided a room for her. But how sad, frightened of her own family. She'd not been able to share all those successes.

How have your studies changed you?

When I went back my third year, from that point on, there was no holding back. I didn't fail after that and it gave me an awful lot of confidence in myself. I'm far more articulate now, although you're probably thinking, what was he like before? But it's far easier to express myself on paper and a lot easier to talk to people. I have confidence in my own ability and also I recognize my limitations. And that's because of the psychology courses I did.

What's been the impact of your studies on your career?

My first year got me interested in psychology. I took a second foundation course in technology because if psychology wasn't going to be successful, with the background I've had in laboratories and environmental health, I could fall back on that. I had a vague plan, it was going to be either very scientific or very psychological. Psychology was my third course and I did quite well. It encouraged me an enormous amount to have my tutor say, I don't give those marks out lightly. I decided to take further courses in psychology and I got eighty per cent pass marks, sometimes ninety, that spurred me on. I thought, maybe the OU is easy. But my tutor in a third-level course had to postpone her marking and she had a colleague in Cambridge mark our assignments instead. A Cambridge don. And I said, That's it, my marks are going to go down. She was quite annoyed and she said what makes you think that because I give you certain marks that they're going to be any different coming from a tutor at Cambridge? And my marks didn't change. I realized then that the OU is a very tough course.

How has continuing your education changed your ideas about work including housework?

I haven't got an entrepreneurial mind so I don't equate success with financial competence. Success in social work is being competent in your job. For example, recently there was a case where two young children were placed for adoption. This was only after every avenue was tried to support the mother, to rehabilitate her, to give her every opportunity and the time to show that she was capable. But there was a cut off point. These were young children. They couldn't wait. And people from outside agencies, the guardian ad litems, the solicitor, legal services, senior officers in social services, judged that my work had been competently carried out. That judgment is success in social work. It's a hell of a responsibility, a hell of a decision to have to make. Social work is to some extent destructive. It does break up families. When you take someone's children away, you've destroyed a part of their life and you can't get away from that.

In our office there's a poster of a man being hung from a tree and there's a crowd of people around, and it says, 'Social worker who took the children away from the family.' And there's an identical poster right next door and it says, 'Social worker who didn't take the children away.' You're damned if you do, and damned if you don't. That's why I want to change to counselling psychology, because while you can't be successful in every case, you can be successful with those people who are able to heal themselves.

As far as housework is concerned, my father always worked, my mother always worked, so they share the housework, hoovering, washing up, getting dinner. They've always mucked in together. And one of the agreements when I went back to college at City and Guilds was that I would iron my own clothes and help with shopping and various things around the house. I was schooled before I got married, and my wife is also a firm believer in dividing things right down the middle. She's not what you'd call a Hausfrau.

How did your studies affect your interests?

I read different types of books now. I read more biographies, whereas before it would have been novels, science fiction, fantasy. I like a good psychological thriller like Dostoyevsky or Tolstoy. I am more interested in the characterisation of a book, the personalities, than I am in the actual story. *Anna Karenina* is a psychological novel as far as I'm concerned and *The Devils*.

My friends now are of academic standard, graduates themselves or like a friend of mine who's a JP and a manager. Your conversation is on an intellectual level, your humour's more subtle. I wouldn't have anything in common with my old friends if I met them. That's sad but inevitable. I can't converse on a mundane, small-talk level with people that I used to be acquainted with.

Why would you recommend continuing education to other men?

Studying alone gives you discipline that you may never have had before. And, most important, a goal. On residential weekends and weeks away, you're with people from wealthy backgrounds, people from quite ordinary backgrounds like me, but they've all got the same goal. You realize that all the fears and hangups you've had about your ability are the same as everybody else's.

It made me value friendships more. When you go off with your private fears and worries and find yourself opening up to other students, you find they are in the same position as you, sometimes worse. You tend to trust the exchange. I would put myself out far more now on an emotional level for a friend. If they're in trouble, I'd let them know I'm there for them if they need me. I value that in people now, it's part of being a friend.

And because the student population is so diverse, you learn things from other students. I graduated with a man eighty years old. Imagine, at his time of life, he had the motivation to do that. He taught me, you should make the most of your life right to the very end. And if you make remarks that aren't politically correct, your fellow students, in a gentle, debating sort of way, correct you. The socialisation with other mature students is very important, because if you go to a self-help group or to the pub after the classroom or to any function, you learn you can have friendships right across society.

The thing is, there are a wealth of people who have the ability to add to this country and yet education is reserved for the privileged. When I went for an exam one day I met this bloke in his bus driver's outfit and I thought, he's bound to know where this hall is because he's a bus driver. And I asked and he said, Hold on, I'm going down there. I'm doing my maths exam. And then he was going to work afterwards. For a lot of people, education is the only thing they've got to live for. In my case, it meant I could go forward job-wise, and not be dissatisfied and unhappy, which you pass on to your family, don't you?

How does continuing education prepare men for change?

By giving them the skills on paper they need to change. The only way you look good on paper is to have qualifications or experience in a certain field. If you want to get into social work or computers or whatever, you may think, I'm self-taught in computers, or I interact well with other people. But unless you can prove it, you won't be given a chance. It took me five years from being made redundant to being worth considering in social welfare. I asked my boss why she hired me, and she said, Because your studies made you look good on paper.

If there were no work except part-time, deadend jobs, would you do that again?

That's frightening but I would do it, for the financial side of it. I could go back to being a drainman. I've done it before, I can do it again. But all the time I was doing it, the thing that runs through your mind is you're being punished. Most certainly my fellow workers felt that way, in environmental health. They had come from skilled jobs. One young fellow had been a maintenance fitter, another fellow'd been a toolmaker.

You feel like you've been bypassed by society. You had a job where you used your skills and now you're of no use to anybody. You feel angry toward the employer for not being competitive enough. Some of the plant machinery we had was Victorian and then you'd go to Germany and they didn't work any harder than we did, but their machinery was far more up to date. The British workforce works four times harder because we have this outdated machinery.

I also felt at the time that the conservative government was out to undermine the working class. You felt, you are expendable. It didn't matter to them that a factory closed. But a factory is a community. When they destroyed our factory, they destroyed local shops and offices, cricket teams, football teams, families that got together, Christmas parties for children, that was part of the work, part of the actual socialisation of seven hundred men and women. This is still happening all over. You feel like that's all you're good for, to do drains. It's a terrible feeling.

What is the biggest social or economic problem today in the UK?

Unemployment and young people, and they're linked. I'm working with parents now who have never had a job. They see themselves as an underclass, and that there's a working society that they aren't a part of. I hate class distinctions. I hate that labeling. But I appreciate that the people I work with see me as radically different from the way I see myself. They see somebody who's got a good job, car, home, security, money. How can they feel I understand their life? Because, I don't suppose I do. I've never been unemployed for any length of time. I don't know what it's like not to work for months, years.

The long-term ill of society is unemployment, because no matter what job you do, there's nothing like the feeling at the end of the week to be paid. Even working with the rain running down my neck, soaked to the skin, pay day was there. I could go and have a pint. I could afford to study. I had pride in myself.

I did some student work with adolescents who were coming out of long-term care into independent living. Some of them had been in prison. They desperately wanted jobs and they were saying to me that their old friends were nicking stereos from cars and that if things didn't change for them soon, they would be doing that. They'd say, I don't want to go back to prison, I hate it, but I need money. I need to have pride in myself. I saw how they could justify stealing to themselves. They saw it as work. They could sell those things and at the end of the day say, I'm my own person.

To be born into obsolescence has got to be the worst possible fate. But it is becoming the fate of more and more men and women. Will the end of paid work spell a death sentence for civilization as we have come to know it, or might we be on the brink of great social-economic transformation?

Chapter 9

Age of the Skills Portfolio

In the past, for most of us, our work portfolio has had only one item in it, at least for men. It was their job or, more grandiosely, their career. This was, when you think about it, a risky strategy. Few would these days put all their money into one asset, yet that is what a lot of us have been doing with our lives. That one asset, that one job, has had to work overtime for we have looked to it for so many things at once— for interest or satisfaction in the work itself, for interesting people and good company, for security and money, for the chance of development...no wonder, in retrospect, that so many have been disappointed (Handy, p.147).

For young people, a portfolio is a piece of cake

`How I describe myself changes depending on who I'm talking to. It's difficult when you start out, because people think of you as just one thing. I think my parents still find it difficult. They're more likely to ask me "how's the BBC" than how my design work is going. That's not because they don't want me to work as a designer, but until I've established myself they still see me as earning my money in research. At one point I was quite disappointed in myself. I thought I was quite a flibbertigibbet, flying around from one thing to another, which is disturbing. Over time I've begun to see that there is a connection. It's all me, and you can see the threads of yourself that run through things.' Even if this young woman's parents don't yet see the threads. The research she refers to is market research, applying a degree in psychology (Aitchison, 1995).

For older people it ain't that easy

If you think (a) the young woman above is a total flake, and (b) naturally, flaky people have all sorts of questionable skills, Charles Handy would say, `Hold on, old man, sooner or later, as the organisation is reshaped, we shall all be portfolio people. Including you. With four main categories of work in your portfolio; paid work and three kinds of free work, home, gift, and study. You'll have to look at parts of yourself you have, as a man, traditionally ignored.'

Handy acknowledges how difficult it is in midlife to change from a one-item portfolio to a multi-item one. His example is William, 48, a senior account director who has been told by the Chairman that he must 'move on' at the end of the year. So William says, I need another job, and Handy asks William what he's good at. He says account advertising. Handy tells him to go away and ask twenty people who know him well, at work or outside work, to tell him one thing they think he does well. In a fortnight William returns with a list of twenty things, not one of which is running an account group. Handy and he discuss various ways in which William can put his many talents to use—business ventures, voluntary activities, teaching, writing. Instead he takes another 'proper job' in another ad agency. But sooner or later, William, and every full-time core employee, will be forced to put into his portfolio such items as fluency in French, experience as a school governor, sailing prowess, lorry driving skills, acting ability, gardening how-to, social skills gained at the Citizens Advice Bureau, you name it.

School children today develop the portfolio mentality through a method of assessment called 'Recording of Achievement and Action Planning.' The basic notion is you review, as you go, what you learn and achieve. You constantly articulate what your goals are, how you're going to achieve those goals, and what new learning you must acquire. In thinking about jobs, you articulate the marketability—for an organisation or working freelance—of the experience and abilities you've gained. You ask, how are my various skills transferable—to a host of different work situations?

Your skills are your market value

Here, from Tom 'In Search of Excellence' Peters (1994), are five pieces of advice for these Years of Living Dangerously: (1) Spend time with your Rolodex, in other words, spend time on the phone cultivating your clients, customers, contacts. (2) Spend time with your friends, networking with your community, neighbours, associations, church. (3) Spend time at daily exercise, hobbies and rituals, cabinetry, cooking, photography. (4) Spend time doing things for laughs, read funny books, see funny movies, go to funny plays. (5) Spend time building your skills. 'Your security is proportional to your market value, and that is proportional to how sharp your skills are. Not getting smarter is seen today as just getting dumber. Just for starters, that means you should be getting to the classroom, by hook or by crook—with or without the company's help. Besides formal classwork, signing up for oddball assignments is the best way to pick up skills. Another surprisingly helpful route: off-the-job volunteer work.'

Long before anyone coined the term 'portfolio', Chapter 9's George Saint was building his. He illustrates the most important fact about a portfolio—it is totally your responsibility. No government, no charitable organisation, no company, no counsellor will, or can, do it for you.

Chapter 10

George Saint and the Lure of Under Ground

Change can come in a minute. Being a union chap, in a `safe' position with the railway for the last 25 years, I know things can't stay status quo. I've done adult education classes, typing skills, how to start a business up. We bought equipment to start our own printing business. I had a license for a public house for three years. Whilst on the railway, myself and a colleague had a decorators business. And I went to Exeter and got a heavy goods lorry license. Now if everything else fails, I can be a very educated lorry driver, Class I, anywhere in the world. Things can suddenly disappear, people's lifestyles can just go out the window. If that happens, I'll pack up a big bag and go.

I recognised George the instant he strode into the shabby student union at the University of East London. In contrast to the teenage crowd, all faded jeans and layers of grunge, George was neatly attired in grey trousers and navy sweater, and carried a white lab coat with his briefcase. He is chubby, bearded, self-assured, and speaks with a rapid fire East End accent. He is now 43 and began the OU at 35. When I saw him he was finishing the third year of a BSc in archaeology.

George's family was working class and he left school at 16 with no O-levels. He has been with London Underground since 1970, starting as a guard, and working as a night ballast train driver during his studies, which he began in 1986. Currently, his job title is transplant duty manager. Transplant is that part of the London Underground network which manages the track, track maintenance, repair. George's wife Linda is a bookbinder and runs an antiques stall. They have a 13-year-old daughter from this, his second marriage.

Your reasons for doing a university degree?

I have always enjoyed studying and another driver and I got talking at our meal break and I mentioned the subjects I was interested in and he showed me what he was reading and it started from there. The railway is a mass of individuals in regard to intellect, ideas, hobbies. But if you haven't got an active hobby or studies, you get a lot of boredom. And with shift work, you've got time to study, especially if you do nights.

I thought, if I'm going to study, there might as well be something at the end of it. In 1986 in terms of part-time, the OU was the only road to go down. I've also been to Oxford for an advanced certificate in archaeology and if you wanted information there, you had to go and look for it. But with the OU, because you didn't have time to go and look for it, everything was given to you in the units. It's my impression that the majority of men do degrees for job-related reasons, men in managerial jobs to get more qualifications, teachers wanting to advance.

What obstacles did you have?

I missed the grammar school by a very small amount and went to Forest Gate High. I was in one of the top forms until my last year. We had a lot of gangs, the Greasers, Mods, and Rockers. I was a Greaser. It was very hard to be a swot and a bit of a lad as well. Most of the chaps I associated with were from the lower forms, but we all went out together to the early Rolling Stones concerts in Hyde Park. There was a lot of chastisement in school, the cane, a clap on the ear. Being a gang, you were always tempted to do something that somebody else wouldn't do. But I always kept up, even though now and again I abused authority, I still kept up doing the work.

So much for my past. But if it wasn't for Linda, I wouldn't have done the degree, because of the daily restrictions on your personal life. Especially when shit happens at work, you've got to come home and disappear upstairs and start studying. There were never any arguments about, Come down here, do this decorating, take Amanda to school, do this, do that. My wife's support was responsible for my success more than my determination. She could have said at any moment, For God's sake, pack it up.

How have your studies changed you?

It has to be time management. As a result of the whole course. As it progressed, you had to be on time, you had to be there. That reflected back on my work on the outside. I learned to get things done on time, in on time, be somewhere on time. Now I dislike loose ends and I make sure things are put in certain places. I also learned to put everything down in writing, and to keep working notes.

What's been the impact of your studies on your career?

Getting into management. I've been in management now for 18 months. I was a union official with a very strong socialist background and now I have a `dead man's shoes job'. That's East End slang for a job where the only way to get it is if somebody dies or retires. It's also a job a person's not likely to leave because of the complexity and the professional aspect to it. It was a good position to get into because I'm working with the same staff I've always worked with. I know their fiddles, and they know I've done exactly the same things. The faces never changed so I didn't have to worry about being taken off a train one morning and becoming a manager amongst entirely different people the next day. You can't put on any airs and grace with these chaps. If you've been driving trains til last Tuesday, you can't suddenly change overnight.

No one course prepared me, simply finishing it. When you leave school and you drive trains, anything you have to write out, it's like, Sorry, I was sick, stomach upset. I'd been out of school for sixteen years, without having to compose a single written report. But after my degree, I felt more than skilled enough to go into the office and do what was required of me. I walked straight in with confidence. Starting with the interview.

What's the most important use you make of your degree?

As a springboard to further education. Especially doing research, you get more attention when you've got a degree. People take notice of you, people listen more to you. With the degree, also, I rediscovered the art of taking notes which mean something, not scribbles I want to avoid afterward. I rediscovered the art of writing essays and having someone say, I can make sense of that, George.

I also learned how to talk in different situations. I talk one way when I go along to the Victoria and Albert Museum Society. Or when I work at the British Museum, where I obviously meet loads of people who are middle class. And if I've just come from college where I've talked to my colleagues about academic topics, I've got to go from one level to another when I go back to the pubs and the clubs where I talk about bowling, football, Coronation Street. Being an East Ender, you relax when you're talking to East Enders in the same old way. And you have to relapse into it, otherwise you're no longer accepted.

What are your educational plans?

I'd like to do a degree with the City University, a geology course, soft rocks or volcanism. I belong to the Geological Association. And the OU Geological Society and God knows how many others. I did attempt to put in for it the year before last, but the wife talked me out of it. Really, she said, get this out of the way first. I have a tendency in the last year of a course to start the first year of another one.

How has continuing your education changed your ideas about work?

I would like personally for people to retire at 40 for twenty years, and then come back at 60 and work until they die. I've seen so many people, especially on the railway, retire at 65, when they're used to getting up at 5 o'clock and being at work at 6, working, laughing and joking, and to suddenly become broken off from that environment, they get depressed, they mentally collapse. They're dead in themselves before they physically die. At forty I think they should have their pension, have their enjoyment, like several years studying, and then go back to work. My father worked until he was 85 and it wasn't til after he retired, that he suddenly went downhill. He had no reason to get up in the morning.

How did your studies affect your interests?

I did an advanced certificate at Oxford in archaeology four years ago. With the Underground there is quite a lot of tunneling work going on and that's why I got interested in geology. We were cutting through a very boring strata in the Thames Basin, but I'd get limestones and granites, bits of flint, coming through for ballast I could paw through. For my current degree I've got exams in June so I'm rushing around to draw bits and pieces together. I've got two more essays to do. One of them's going to be published in one of the local periodicals.

And since the course, when we get away in our caravan to Europe, when you stop somewhere, you don't look up in the sky and at the lovely scenery, you look at what the scenery consists of, the different forms of strata, different rock formations. I would love to go to Iceland, lot of geology there, it's a living island.

Have your values changed since the OU?

You start pigeon holing people your first year on the course. You think this bloke, he knows everything, and that old bloke, he knows nothing. And you think, I've got this silly question to ask, but I'm not going to ask it. But you go along, and this chap, who sounds as though he knows everything, he asks a question that you think is ten times more stupid than yours. And this old bloke over here gives him the answer. So I learned not to pigeon hole people.

My daughter's education has since become very important to me. She got into secondary school last year, Tower Hamlets Raines Foundation School, which has always been grant-maintained, since the 1700s. My daughter comes home and she enjoys that school, she wakes up in the morning and wants to go to that school.

I think it's really worth it for parents today to look into the best school for their child. If one or two children don't get on at a school, I say, okay, it's the individual children, they probably have their troubles outside as well. But a majority of students at many schools are dissatisfied. The staff as well. So you've got to go outside. I am so relieved that it worked out. Because we received a rejection letter initially saying they weren't taking anybody from outside the borough. I could have broken into tears and I apologized to my daughter, it meant so much to her. A week later I drove past and I thought, those so and so's. I got home about half past seven and the first post had been and there was a letter from Raines. It was, Dear Mr and Mrs Saint, It is our pleasure to inform you that a vacancy has arisen and we're giving it to Amanda. I went over the moon. I shouted up the stairs and woke the whole household up.

Why would you recommend continuing education to other men?

You've got to have a target. The BA gave me a target. The BSc is obviously a target. If you don't study, you're going to stay status quo. When you're studying, you've got to meet deadlines, you've got your essays, your exams, and the final exam. The targets have got to be ones you know you can reach, not targets way above your head, and ones that you want to reach, not ones you're obliged to do, like in the work environment. Like I'm forced to take management training courses within the railway.

How do you like your change to manager?

I'm enjoying the change because I'm carrying on, I'm still George Saint, I'm nobody different. I didn't have to go elsewhere, as I said earlier, where I'd have to lay the law down. And I get to look after my men. Let a bloke know when he's done a good job. Thank him. Go and slap a bloke on the back and say, Well done. That means more than any £5 pay raise. But the changes over the last five years can make you so depressed. These innovations will work in a biscuit factory or work in an aircraft manufacturing place, but they won't work on a social industry such as the railway where everybody works together. Because at the end of the day, it's not 500 aircraft parts produced or sixteen cars. At the end of the day it's that the service is still running and running well. And it's a service that needs to be subsidised.

The top railway bosses have been railway men in the past. Today they're academics or businessmen looking for a profit. If you're a biscuit company employee or a car manufacturing employee, then you're doing a job. But when you're a railwayman, you spend more time on the railway than you spend with your family. And when something happens to it and you've got no say in it, you feel so despondent. More should be put into looking after the man on the platform and short-term contracts aren't a very good idea. Those people have got no great commitment towards it. Okay, they can be cheaper than us, but only on paper. If we put the infrastructure in and do it wrong, we go back the following day and fix it. But with contractors, we've got no recall. They can disappear.

How does continuing education prepare men for change?

If you go to work each day and you don't have any other interests, you come home, sit indoors, watch telly and go out to the pub. Holidays and Christmas are the only things to look forward to, the peaks. You become very mundane and to change would be the hardest thing in the world for you.

But when you've got a target, an enjoyable educational target, you want to keep on til you reach it. If I got into a subject and I couldn't understand it, I wasn't going to give up. And if I got things wrong, I'd erase the thoughts from my mind and start again on the right channel. This process changes you. I can talk to people of some standing about any subject now and have no cause to back out of the conversation or walk away at a dinner party or social function. I've become that self-confident.

If the work world won't stay status quo, then men can't stay status quo. More important, there's got to be more to life than your job, otherwise like George's father, if you have no home work or gift work or study work to get up for, retirement could mean you die.

Chapter 11

Age of Early Retirement

Life used to begin at 40. But these days, as far as employers are concerned, you virtually have one foot in the grave...you are nearly past it. A survey published last year...found that 42 was the point at which most people said ageism in the workplace began to bite. Two-thirds of employees surveyed said that they had been excluded from job interviews or offers because of age.... Paul Gregg, an economist at the London School of Economics, estimates that most people have one promotion left in them after the age of 40— and then they are out. The story goes that in most companies, once you are over 50, you can either be chairman or clean the toilets (O'Sullivan, 1996).

The truth about early retirement

When Charles Handy got his first job thirty years ago he signed on for 100,000 hours of work in his lifetime. He reckoned if he worked 47 hours a week for 47 weeks a year for 47 years of his life, it would be 100,000 hours, give or take a few. His children, however, a generation later can expect their jobs to add up to 50,000 hours. The kids have four principal options for putting in those 50,000 hours. One, they could work 45 hours a week for 45 weeks a year for 25 years. If they start working at age 25, you can see retirement age has gone down to 50. Two, they could work 25 hours a week for 45 weeks of the year (part-time), or three, 45 hours a week for 25 weeks a year (temporary) for 45 years. Whether they do temporary or part-time work, the sum is still $25 \times 45 \times 45 = 50,000$ hours. But obviously retirement age goes way up. It also goes up with a fourth option of working full-time for ten years, then taking ten years out to raise a family, then returning to work fifteen more years full-time. So, it looks like only a minority of workers are going to 'retire early', the core elite of professionals, managers, and skilled technicians.

The incredible shrinking career

For a few men in the core elite, life in fact begins at forty. More and more guys in their early forties are being thrust into the eminent positions that in the past were the reserve of men in their fifties and sixties. To quote the 42-year-old chief executive of Barclays Banks: `The jobs have become infinitely more demanding in the past ten years because of the rate at which businesses change. The idea that at the top of a business, life was very stable and what you most needed to run it was wisdom—that's really been turned upside-down. What you need now in a business is energy, which would have seemed a horrific idea 20 years ago (Sieghart, 1994).'

What are these youthful CEOs going to do when they hit fifty? Some will slide easily into the portfolio mode and go forth to earn a good living in consultancy, part-time chairmanships and directorships. Others will go into unpaid work like Jimmy Winterfloor, former product manager of a confectionery firm, made redundant after 27 years. First Mr. Winterfloor tried finding another paid job but `No one was interested in someone who had maybe 10 years' work left in them. They wanted someone younger, who would in time fill senior positions.' So he volunteered to work for British Executive Services Overseas and reports `I've been all over the world. I'm just back from Bangladesh, where I was sorting out management problems in a biscuit and bread company. Developing countries revere people over 50 who have a lifetime of experience. I would rather give my knowledge away for nothing to someone who appreciates it than sit at home in a country that does not seem to want it.' He's put his finger on the culprit behind this Age of Early Retirement, age discrimination (O'Sullivan, 1996).

The prejudice that a person's age determines whether they can do a particular job is very widespread and socially acceptable in Britain. Advert after newspaper advert tell older people they need not apply. The stereotype is that young people have more energy and drive and cut through the detail faster. And that older people are less flexible, going in a straight line, not taking any risks. So one group of losers in the 1990s is men in their fifties who spent their early years doing boring jobs but looking forward to the rewards of seniority. Now `change management' has pulled those rewards out from under them.

Early retirement is not the right word for some

Charles Handy in *The Age of Unreason* maintains that many a person is heard to boast today of how they `managed to arrange early retirement'. `Ask those people what they will do next and they do not talk of wage work but of...time for old enthusiasms, or new causes and hobbies (gift work), of helping out more with household chores or parenting (homework) or of taking up a new interest (study work). They don't call it work, but they should. They are building up a new portfolio and in so doing re-defining their lives and themselves (p. 150).'

One of this breed is Handy's old friend Paul Anderson. His answerphone replies `Anderson Associates' and gives another number. Handy laughs, `I know that the Associates are he and his wife and occasional friends in his or her multifarious little enterprises, some of which make money, many of which don't. *I* know that the other telephone number is a fishing lodge...*I* know that his wife, a freelance journalist since the children grew up, makes more money than him, that their kitchen is their office. *I know that he would never go back to working in a bank, that the telephone and the new opportunities for little service enterprises have transformed both their lives (p.67).'*

As Mahmood Tootoonchian's story next reveals, however, for a midlife degree to lead to employment, much, much more must go into the portfolios of men who will face age discrimination. There must be additional training courses, lots of volunteer experiences, and much networking around one's community to explain one's skills to a wide range of contacts. Plus the same perseverance that went into pursuing the degree.

Chapter 12

Mahmood Tootoonchian, Who Retired to Develop Himself

There are other things in life, apart from money, which make life much more meaningful. To be able to care for other people, be useful to other people, do something worthwhile for other people either educationally or financially, be supportive when others are in need. Life is very short and no matter how much money we make, we won't be remembered for it. But if we did something good, built a hospital or wrote a useful book, these are the things we will be remembered for.

I asked Mahmood to meet me at Parsifal College in Finchley thinking it might be familiar to an OU Region 01 student. I was right. While I was taken aback by the bewildering maze of corridors and classrooms and the bustle of crowds of students, Mahmood was right at home.

Everything about Mahmood is cautious, deliberate, and dignified. He was dressed sombrely in black and navy and carefully arranged his overcoat, scarf, pens and glasses cases, before easing himself into a chair and politely asking me to review for him the purpose of the interview.

Mahmood was born in 1934 in Hamadan, Iran. His family was middle-class and his father was a merchant of tobacco and that's why his name is Tootoonchian. 'Tootoon' is Persian for tobacco. Mahmood is now a British citizen and is married with two grown children, a daughter 33, and a son 25. He is a Shi'ite Muslim. He started the OU in 1983 at the age of 48 with the arts foundation course and graduated in 1993, having concentrated in psychology.

Mahmood, which means 'pleasant,' graduated from Abadan Technical Institute in 1954 with a diploma in commerce and began working for the National Iranian Oil Company as a personnel clerk. He was translator and reporter for the company magazine, and spent ten years in Training and Development where he taught English and headed Language and Commercial Training. He worked a total of 27 years for NIOC and its successor, retiring 'early' at age 46 from personnel management.

Your reasons for doing a university degree?

I always wanted to get a degree in psychology. It was a really strong desire. I used to read psychological books when I was in Iran, in Persian, of course, at the time. So I retired early to continue my study of psychology and achieve my dream. Also, I hoped a degree would somehow enhance my chances of employment. But it didn't, because of my age.

What obstacles did you have?

English was not a problem, because when I was a child of seven years old I wished that I would be either a doctor or a teacher of English. I didn't become a doctor because I enrolled in a technical institute and completed a commercial course, so I had to follow a commercial career. But I made my other wish come true by studying English and becoming competent in English, and later, when a post of teacher of English opened in the training department of the NIOC, I was selected for that post. I taught English for almost ten years at different levels, including a course in report writing. There came a day when I was promoted to the head of Language and Commercial Training, but there was not much scope in actual teaching of English after that. And then I was transferred to Tehran and I had other jobs, like I used to lead supervisory and management conferences.

Isolation was an obstacle. If I had been studying at a normal university where you would sign up for a course, join the class with the professor or tutor, and stay with it for a semester or for a year, it would have been much easier. With distance learning, all the burden is on the shoulders of the student. Study groups started at different times, but after one or two sessions they would break up because people couldn't set the time aside. I came across ladies who lived in small villages and somehow they had the time and the opportunity and the urgent desire to get together and study. But I had to study on my own.

That's why summer school was so important to me because not only was it a very good revision, but I had the chance to ask questions and interact with the students and tutors. They would break the whole group into small groups and you would stay with that group the whole time. We studied together long hours, starting at nine and finishing up at eight, sometimes ten. And since we were all living on one campus, we socialised more. I wasn't lonely there, I must say, because you are bound to meet people. We did everything together and I didn't miss a thing.

How have your studies changed you?

The most important thing was that it was an objective that I had decided to accomplish. Each year I would select a goal for myself, work towards it, solve the problems if there were any, study for it hard, and prepare myself for the examination, and when the 25th of December came and my letter of success came, that gave me a lot of boosting in life. I was proud of myself that I was doing something useful. It makes a better man of you. I felt more lively, I felt like a winner, and that had a positive effect on my family life. In turn, my family and friends were supportive and praised me and that again meant a lot to me. We all went to the graduation ceremony at Wembley Conference Centre. I was accompanied by my wife, daughter, and son, and they took lots of pictures and my daughter took a video film of me which we show to everybody. I even took it to Iran and all my family there watched it.

What's been the impact of your studies on your career?

If I were living in Iran, I'm sure, I would be working as a teacher of English or a translator, using my many years of experience. Here there isn't that much chance for a 59-year-old man. But studying gave me an objective, broadened my knowledge, improved my English, and could have enhanced my chances of getting employment if we didn't have this recession. In fact, I made a couple of attempts to get a job teaching English as a second language here, but they told me the art of teaching English had changed so much that I would have to take a course, in a way start from the very beginning.

What's the most important use you make of your degree?

When I'm reading a book or an article, I can't help but realize that my courses help me to comprehend it better. It was all gain, there was no loss in it at all. And isn't the main objective of studying, development? That's enough. It has given me a chance to develop.

I recently started to translate some articles. I do translation from English into Persian. I recently translated an article on Kafka and I sent it to Tehran to be published in a local magazine. When I was in Iran, I used to do a lot of translations for a magazine called *Management Today*, which used to be published by the state-management sector. And I translated a book on report writing, technical as well as normal report writing. I couldn't do much translation work while I was working on the degree, but that's one way I occupy myself now.

What are your educational plans?

If I take another course at third-level then I would be eligible for an honours BA, so I may do that some day. But when I finished the BA, I intentionally gave myself some space to read, because when you are taking a course, you get stuck in that material and you don't get much opportunity to do general reading. I'd like to do two years of general reading before going back for a third-level course.

How has continuing your education changed your ideas about work?

Success does not have to be financial or in a job. I have always had goals and worked to achieve them. I enjoy self-development, but to succeed on your own, you've got to be self-disciplined. You've got to have an objective, work towards it, solve the problems as they arise, believe that you will succeed, and believe that what you are doing is right. All these things create an atmosphere of success. Once I had slipped a disc and I had to stay in bed 24 hours a day for three months and I was taking a third-level social psychology course. But I didn't give up. I did my course work and wrote my TMAs while I was lying down. I got all my TMAs sent in and I passed that course with very good marks.

How did your studies affect your interests?

I enjoyed the arts foundation very much because I had two very good tutors who introduced us to philosophy, literature, psychology, religious studies, and the arts. It was very useful because it gave us the scope of other courses that one could choose from. It was also good because we met often, almost every week. When the class was over, we used to go to the pub and drink together and talk together, students and tutors, while with my other courses, after tutorials everybody scattered.

I always have been interested in the theatre but there is no question that I go to the theatre in the city more as a result of the Shakespeare course. If it's a good play, my daughter and I make sure that we go to it. And when I see the plays that I covered in the course, they give me much more pleasure now. What have I done most recently? Enjoyed the film *Prospero's Books* and the ballet, *The Nutcracker*.

The OU broadened my scope in life. When you read an article in the paper or a book, you understand it better. When you see a film, the difference between a 12th class diploma and a degree, is that you get more out of it. That is the whole idea of going to the university.

We went to Turkey on our way to Iran this year, Istanbul. And naturally before we went, I studied books and brochures, and I earmarked to visit the beautiful mosques, museums, the bazaar, the two famous bridges. And even though our stay was short, I accomplished most of that. Fortunately, my wife has similar interests.

What was most important in your life before and after the degree?

Before it was my work and my family, and afterward, it is my family and my life. I retired with the idea of developing myself. Staying in touch with my family and friends in Iran is also important. I go to Iran almost every year for about a month. I've got a sister and a brother there, nephews and nieces in Tehran, and we have lots of friends in Iran scattered all over. But I don't see myself moving back in the foreseeable future. I don't have much at stake in Iran. My family are the most important people to me and they're with me here.

Why would you recommend continuing education to other men?

It is a very good thing to do in retirement. I used to get up very early every morning to study and when I had exams, I spent more time studying during the day. I have a very understanding wife, and it made a difference that my daughter would encourage me and would help me if necessary. If I had not been studying I would have found something else to do. But perhaps I would have argued with my wife more. Look at it from this angle. Some men retire at an early age and stay at home and do nothing, and especially if their wives do not work outside the home, they argue all the time and sometimes their marriages are destroyed. While the opposite happened as far as we were concerned. I would say my wife and I have a fairly traditional marriage, but I've taken to helping her more. Sometimes I lay the table, I wash the dishes, and if we are having a small party, I help her with the work and looking after the guests.

And I must say, that from studying the psychology courses, I did treat my children more appropriately. For instance, when my son said some harsh words about the young men who vandalize the telephone box or some other nearby property, I explained to him *why* they would do this. Instead of taking the official view and blaming these youngsters as bad people, I took the view that it's related to the situation in which they live, their culture, and it clarified the situation for my son so that he would no longer treat it with prejudice.

I've had no problem with what to do with my time, but then I retired at an early age when I had lots of energy. I've not yet reached the actual retirement age of 65, and I don't know if I'll have the same energy on that date. The people with whom I socialise are all working and much younger than I am. We get together every other week and they live mostly in my neighborhood. We meet in different people's houses. A friend of mine would give a party at which there would be some new faces and I'd meet someone interesting, we'd invite him to our place or they'd invite us to their place, and that's how we broaden our circle of friends. I am more comfortable with my Iranian friends.

What changes might Iranian culture offer British culture?

It's the whole of Western culture that we have something to add to. And it's not only my country that could contribute, but the East. Western culture has become very money-oriented, while we think that there are other aspects of life which have more meaning. Naturally, we all need something to live on and would like to live comfortably, and for that we have got to earn money, no question about that. But we have got a very rich source of spiritual writing, such as the writings of Molana Jaleledin Mowlavi, Sheikh Moslehedin Saadi Shiraz, Khajeh Mohammad Hafez Shirazi, Omar Khayam. I study the works of these people all the time. Even illiterate Iranians know by heart some of the poems of Saadi and Hafez. Their work gives me inspiration and the opportunity to remember that life is not all money, and that there are more important and more useful things in life. Iranians as a whole are a very hospitable and warm-hearted and they mostly have an unmaterialistic view on life. Perhaps these qualities of being kind and caring are why we tend to stick together.

As we walked out of Parsifal College into the gray gloom and chill of a February afternoon, Mahmood exuberantly described a city he said I must get to someday, Isfahan, south of Tehran, midway between the Caspian Sea and the Persian Gulf, east of the Zagros Mountains. It's his favorite. It's on my list, Mahmood, it's on my list.

Chapter 13

A Crisis in Men's Health

Employment trends are not conducive to better health. While one in 10 men has no job at all, many of those in work do the job of two. "Excessive employment demands promote physical and psychological ill-health and discourage early action to resolve problems," says Dr Surawy, who has noticed increasing levels of stress in the past few years among his male patients. "With a work culture in which only the fittest survive, no one will admit to weakness." Meanwhile, in a society which has not yet accepted that breadmaker can be as valid a male role as breadwinner, evidence continues to accumulate showing that lack of a job destroys masculine self-esteem and undermines health (Stepney, 1996).

You've already learned that Britain's workers are the sick men of Europe, costing the UK economy £15 billion a year in time off due to sickness and injury. You've already learned that life expectancy is two years longer in Europe than in Britain, and that young men with no money and no work are increasingly killing themselves. Another fact is that the biggest gaps between death rates of women and men are between the ages of 15 and 30, and between the ages of 55-70. Both transitional work ages.

I was hoping to find a giant link between higher education and job satisfaction and men taking better care of themselves. I didn't, but here are some things to think about to answer the question, why do men pay fewer than half the visits women make to their GPs?

Is seeking help unmanly, perhaps?

If men are missing so much work for sickness, you'd expect surgeries to be crowded with them. But either guys are doctoring themselves, or deluding themselves, because they won't see a doc until a serious problem develops and even then they need a woman pushing them.

Even when Haringey Borough opened a health information stall for men in a shopping mall, 50 per cent of its customers were women—mothers worried about sons, wives worried about husbands, daughters worried about fathers. Haringey's Well Man Clinic closed after a year because of lack of attendance.

Men wouldn't go because 'It doesn't do to know too much because it can frighten you,' 'Ignorance is bliss,' and 'What puts me off is fear of what I might find out.' Men are really good at denial. The situation is so bad that much health education for men is targeted at women, in the hope that they will pass it on (Jane Smith, 1994).

Are men's stereotypes of male strength and fitness to blame? Are men so detached from their feelings and bodies that they don't notice danger signals? Seriously, is being sick unmanly?

Getting emotional certainly is, unmanly

It's okay to express feelings and emotions if you're a woman, but men are conditioned not to. Without the social networks women have where they vent their negative feelings, men fall into outlets such as acting out, alcohol and drug abuse, suicide, and death by untreated diseases such as lung cancer, heart disease, and prostate cancer. It's no accident that John Walker, a social worker, someone you'd expect to be in touch with his feelings, was the first to successfully sue his employers (£175,000 damages) for ill health caused by overwork. He suffered two nervous breakdowns which he was not afraid to admit and take to court where he proved they were caused by agency understaffing.

Another casualty of overwork was MP Stephen Milligan. Emma Nicholson said his death casts a shadow over the way the whole House of Commons works: 'How can you possibly expect people who work 18-20 hours a day, nearly seven day a week, to have any sort of comfortable and happy life outside?' Suzanne Moore (1994), pondering the impersonal nature of men's friendships, asked why men couldn't occasionally, for their own good, talk to one another about things that really matter, personal things—like emotions, like feeling depressed?

And a man with an emotionally-related illness?

As many as one in five people suffers from a digestive disturbance which could be diagnosed as IBS (Irritable Bowel Syndrome). And nine times out of ten, IBS is linked with stress. And, says a counselling psychologist, 'the increase in stress since the recession has been tremendous, and, as a consequence, there has been a massive increase in IBS—particularly among teachers, people working in banking and insurance and manual workers. It's like a 20th-century plague.'

But men get very cross when it's suggested that (a) their intestinal problems have an emotional component, (b) their famed British stiff upper lip is at the heart of the problem, and (c) the best way to treat their unhappiness and tension is talk, talk, talk (Rowlands, 1996).

Worried sick by work

A Harris survey found, not surprisingly, that British workers suffer more stress-related illnesses than any of their European counterparts. Nearly 60% of British workers complain of stress compared with a European average of 54%. One in five British workers has taken time off because of work worries, costing companies £525 a year per employee. Frequent complaints include headaches, long-term tiredness, backache, depression and anxiety, and, of course, IBS. So, let's accept these grim statistics, but end on a positive note with four ways for men to take responsibility for their health: (1) Accept deep-down in your mind and body that jobs are no longer for life. (2) Keep your skills sharp through networking and taking training courses. Don't rely on your company or anybody else. Look for courses yourself. (3) Develop lots of outside interests— play a musical instrument, join a local society, become a school governor. Outside interests give you an identity independent of your job. (4) Take up physical exercise regularly which brings a sense of well-being (Hadley, 1994).

————————————

Gay men find it easier than straight men to express personal needs, seek help quickly from the health services, and depend on a social support network when they're hurting. One is nurse Michael Moore of Chapter 14 whose job, always secure because nurses are in such short supply, has gained in satisfaction as Michael has added qualification after qualification to his portfolio. His health is further insured by a stable, long-term relationship, a big, comfortable home in a small town, and lots of sunshine beach holidays.

Chapter 14

Michael Moore, Who Finally Got Into Computers

One other thing my degree has done is I've recently been appointed honorary lecturer in nursing at Birmingham University. Which means I get to teach brand new students, who are doing the university nursing course, basic practical skills. Bedbathing patients, taking temperatures, pulses, blood pressures, caring for somebody's pressure areas, getting patients up out of bed very quickly. Up to now my teaching has been with post-registration, high-level, qualified staff. So the change is very stimulating.

Michael Moore lives in Ross-on-Wye in a rambling Victorian house where we were introduced to his partner, Don, an ambulance technician, and their ancient cat, Sam, who now sleeps 23 hours a day. Don disappeared to do the shopping and then to fix a scrumptious lunch while Cliff Lunneborg explored the paths by the river. Michael and I settled into cat-clawed overstuffed period furniture in the parlor for our interview.

Michael's youthful face, ready smile, and gentle, soft-spoken manner bely his age of 42. He was born in Manchester, his family was working class, and he left school with several CSEs but no O-levels. At 21 he completed a three-year SRN hospital training program. He began his BA studies in 1986 concentrating in social science. He has completed a PGCE teacher training course at the University of Greenwich so that he is a qualified nurse tutor in addition to being training manager in charge of all clinical and non-clinical training at his Birmingham hospital.

Your reasons for doing a university degree?

I was in charge of the hospital at night and I felt I could do the job backwards. I told the director of nursing I was bored but that I didn't want to leave. She suggested I do an Open University degree. She'd started one herself and had dropped out but she was always recommending it. I thought, I'll explore this, and I did and I never looked back. I didn't have any set plan but I wanted to see myself in my gown and cap. It was to be an affirmation. I wanted to do the courses that I enjoyed doing rather than follow any particular profile so I literally chose on a year to year basis.

What obstacles did you have, particularly early educational obstacles?

Years ago teachers were very negative, telling us things that we could not do, rather than being positive about what we could do. I told the careers master that I wanted to work with computers. I'd heard of these machines and I thought, that is the way to go. The careers master came back with, Your head's in the clouds, Michael. You can go work in an office, you can go work in a factory, or the armed services. That was it. Those were our options.

Between sixteen and eighteen I had a variety of jobs. I had no idea what I wanted to do. I did apply for a social work program that was on-the-job training, but I was too late for that academic year, and the letter from social services said, why not try nursing? I'd never even thought about nursing. My school was streamed and I was in the top stream for quite a number of years so I supposed I had the ability. Now that I'm a teacher myself I can see how important it is to be positive with students. My hospital classes at the moment are discussing the advice we were given by teachers when we left school. The female members of staff weren't advised to go for a career. They were told they'd be getting married and having families. That was some time ago, but the memory is fresh in their minds.

In terms of presentday obstacles, there were none. Don, my partner, was very supportive and everyone at work was always asking me questions about it. I used to go in and spout off what I had learnt the week I'd been off. I used to work seven nights on and seven nights off, so I had to do all my studying in my seven nights off. Actually, that made the first three years of study easy. I never asked for financial support although I'm sure the hospital would have given it. I wanted to do this myself, and I started off with the arts foundation course which certainly wasn't relevant to my job.

How have your studies changed you?

I lost the tunnel vision I used to have. I'm more open to other people's arguments, to looking at things from different points of view. I'm less parochial but also more argumentative. I don't immediately accept what people say. I like to challenge.

A lot of the employees and students at the hospital are Brummie, born and bred. All they know is their area of Birmingham, they don't know what goes on in the rest of the wide world, but still they have very strong views and don't waiver. For example, we have a difficult member of staff who does a good job but there's a lot of criticism aimed at him because, instead of prioritizing his work load and realizing that some jobs are more important than others, he'll say I can't do that because I'm busy doing this. And he feels he's right.

I understand the background that he's come from, and how he's come through the system, so I respect his opinion and might say, in a nice way, maybe you could look at your work from this other, priority point of view? I'm not a didactic sort of teacher, you must do this, you must do that. The Changing Britain, Changing World course did the most to put things in perspective because we explored how people and places are interdependent and cannot survive without the other. And how what applies at the micro level in a small town like this applies to the macro level in the world.

When I got appointed as a clinical instructor, I felt I needed the confidence that knowledge about adult learning would give me, so I took a City and Guilds course in Adult Further Education. Although I felt very confident teaching nurses about clinical methods, I needed more about the psychology of teaching, different approaches to supporting your students, how different people learn at different speeds.

One technique at City and Guilds was we had to do 10-minute presentations in front of trainee teachers. Before my first talk I was petrified. I gathered loads and loads of stuff together and walked around the house reading it out, trying to memorize it. I had no problems doing half-hour clinical sessions with nursing staff, but it was a milestone for me, presenting to a strange group of people. As the course went on, presentations became more and more common, and I just got on with it. Then the hospital training manager left and I was asked to take on a coordinating role, so I was clinical instructor coordinating training for the rest of the hospital. After four months, they offered me the training manager's job.

Can you give me an example of your degree's impact on your career?

Perhaps because of that careers master I had a great fear of computers. I used to go into shops and look at these kids clicking away at the keyboards and think, Gosh, what are they doing? So I decided to do Information Technology. I got a computer on loan and I remember coming in from work one day and this big package had been delivered to our door. I was overwhelmed but Don had no problem putting it all together. He has a knack with that sort of thing even though it was his first computer too.

Having Don around to interpret what the books were telling me to do on the computer made it possible. In learning a practical skill, I find it easier to be shown rather than reading about it in a book. When the computer had to go back, we went out and bought another and we've kept adding to it. We're into Information Technology in a big way. We have our own modem and fax machine. It helps in my job because we're linked to CompuServe which has these huge data bases linked up to Boston Hospital and I have all this information from these data bases at my fingertips. People phone me up now, Mike, we've got a problem with our computer. There are some things I can sort out, others I can't. Then I pick up the phone and say, Don, we've got this problem.

What's the most important use you make of your degree?

I'm using my degree as the tutor-counsellor for a group of nurses who had a two-year course and are converting over to become SRN nurses with three years of course work. They're doing it through a two-year open learning course. We had been sending students who were converting to other hospitals in Birmingham which cost £20,000 just to convert one student. We had to pay their course fees, salaries while they were out of our hospital, and replace them as nursing staff. Obviously we needed a more cost-effective way of training staff and this open learning conversion course came along. With me being trained to be a tutor, I can take on the students. In fact, my first student just passed her exams.

I'm also regarded as something of an all-round resource person at the hospital, not just to the medical staff. Because of all the different subjects I studied, people are always asking, can you come along and advise on this, on that?

What are your educational plans?

Since I did a Health and Disease course, I no longer think scientific medicine is the be all and end all. I'm now interested in alternative therapies so I've enrolled in a college in Manchester where I am doing a weekend course in hypnotherapy. The introduction lasted six weekends and the second part goes from February to August, another weekend course, which is more psychology-orientated. I've had it in the back of my mind that I might have a practice. I've done psychiatric nursing and I'd like to help people with psychological problems. Hypnotherapy is another tool I can sometimes use.

My boss has offered to support my doing a master's degree in training next. It's a distance learning package from Leicester University. Also in my mind is to study herbalism. Education is something I've got to keep doing. I've got to keep myself professionally updated, read my journals and attend lectures regularly. Doing the OU degree and seeing the diversity of the ages of the students made me realize there is no age limit to carrying on studying.

How has continuing your education changed your ideas about work?

As far as redundancy goes, I've always known I would have a job no matter what happened to the economy. As far as job success goes, I'm not bothered about hierarchy or status, although status is nice to have. But I wouldn't mind if I were put back up on the wards, helping patients. I could adapt to that with no problem because what is important to me is caring for people.

Each day I see people get better and that's a very good stimulant for my job. And yes, I see patients die, and that's very sad. But it has made me realize that we're not going to be here all the time and I've got to enjoy life, do things that I want to do. My colleague on night duty, she worked opposite me, we were very close, she died recently of cancer. She was only one year older than me and it's devastating to realize somebody my age is no longer here.

As far as job stress goes, I have always been emotionally open because of the job that I do. In my early days in nursing, we were not allowed to show emotions with patients. We weren't allowed to touch patients for reassurance. But even then, say working in intensive care with patients who were very poorly and relatives who needed my help, I'd put my arms around anybody, male or female, to comfort them, and I didn't find it difficult to cry with someone when their loved one died. So while nursing is very demanding, you can relieve your stress on the job.

That said, I love my vacations. That's why the house is in a state. We're planning a trip to Australia in three weeks time. We like sunshine so we've been to Australia a few times, Goa a couple of times. It's wonderful just lying on the beach and doing nothing. We've been to France quite a few times. I really do like a restful, beach holiday.

How did your studies affect your interests?

We studied the pre-Raphaelites in the arts foundation course. I'd never looked at a picture the way they taught us to look at a picture. So I'm very lucky because Birmingham Art Gallery's got a big collection of pre-Raphaelite paintings. We also studied religious architecture so I can't go anywhere now without looking at churches and how the different ones were fitted into place in the culture of the time here in England. Before I'd just walk down the street and have no consideration for the buildings around me.

What was most important in your life before and after the degree?

Certainly home was before, and now I thoroughly enjoy my job, so home *and* job are now most important. Home is somewhere you can flop down and totally relax. Home is also place. This town is a nice place to live. It's within easy access to several good cities, Gloucester, Hereford, Cheltenham, Bristol. The house itself is very unusual with a genuine Victorian conservatory at the front. We bought it eight years ago and one of the reasons was that bad patch at work I was going through, when I needed a change. So we left a little cottage we had a couple of miles out of town and took this house because if I gave up nursing, we thought it would make a nice coffee shop or art gallery, so we bought it with the possibility that we could start a business here.

Why would you recommend continuing education to other men?

It's getting different people's perspectives that is so amazing. For example, on my Health and Disease course when we looked at the medicalization of birth. Here I am a nurse and I finally realized that while some women are very happy with every piece of machinery you attach to their bodies when they're giving birth, some women are not. And we should respect those wishes, wishes to have a midwife organising and attending the birth. Wishes not to be given any painkiller at all, when we typically pump them full of every painkiller we've got because they're in so much pain.

And you learn that Black people have a different perspective than whites and that history has always been from a white middle-class perspective, and that we've not looked at it from a female point of view or a Black British point of view. Continuing your education makes men think about these other perspectives. It makes you more conscious, more aware, of the variety of ways of looking at things in our society.

As we waved goodbye to Michael and Don from the steamy windows of the bus back to Gloucester, I remarked to Cliff that I was sure most men had no idea how interesting a career in nursing could be. I'll take this up again in Chapter 25.

Chapter 15

The State We're In For

> The ranks of the unemployed and underemployed are growing daily in North America, Europe, and Japan. Even developing nations are facing increasing technological unemployment as transnational companies build state-of-the-art high-tech production facilities all over the world, letting go millions of laborers who can no longer compete with the cost efficiency, quality control, and speed of delivery achieved by automated manufacturing.... Everywhere men and women are worried about their future. The young are beginning to vent their frustration and rage in increasing antisocial behavior. Older workers, caught between a prosperous past and a bleak future, seem resigned, feeling increasingly trapped by social forces over which they have little or no control. Throughout the world there is a sense of momentous change taking place— change so vast in scale that we are barely able to fathom its ultimate impact. Life as we know it is being altered in fundamental ways (Rifkin, p.5)

Hutton's thirty/thirty/forty society

Before we get to Jeremy Rifkin's worldwide nightmare scenario, let's get the employment facts about the UK firmly in mind. To Will Hutton, that first 30 in our 30/30/40 society represents the percentage of *absolutely disadvantaged*. Altogether some 28 per cent of the adult working population are either unemployed or economically inactive. Add in one per cent on government unemployment schemes and do not include anybody who does any part-time work at all, and you've got 30 per cent of the UK working population— absolutely disadvantaged.

The second 30 per cent are the *marginalised insecure*. These people work at part-time and casual jobs that are poorly protected and carry few benefits. It includes persons self-employed for less than two years and temps. It also includes full-timers for less than two years and full-timers who earn less than 50 per cent of the average wage. It does not include the 15 per cent of the population who have held part-time jobs for more than five years.

They go in the 40 per cent *privileged* group, along with full-time employees and the self-employed who have held their jobs for over two years. Most people in trade unions are considered privileged.

The marginalised insecure move between unemployment, self-employment and insecure work. Two-thirds of all new jobs offered the unemployed are part-time or temporary. Only ten per cent of the insecure 30 per cent move to full-time employment. That's the state we're in.

The *state we're in for* is even grimmer. In a survey of corporate leaders from six leading industrial nations, British businesses reported *more* downsizing and corporate restructuring in the past two years than any other country. And they said it would accelerate in the years ahead (Rifkin, 1996). So the stage is set for the remainder of this book. How are we going to turn the Dark Age of Uncertainty into the Bright Age of Cooperative Communities?

First, to help a little bit, a shorter workweek

A shorter workweek has got to happen. It does work. Production has tripled at Hewlett-Packard's Grenoble plant where management adopted a four-day workweek, but keeps the plant running 24 hours a day, seven days a week. Employees are paid the same wages they received working a 37.5-hour week, but now they work either a 26.8-hour night shift, a 33.5-hour afternoon shift, or a 34.7-hour morning shift. When Digital Equipment offered workers a four-day workweek with a seven per cent pay cut, more than 13 per cent of the workforce opted for it. Their action saved jobs that would have been cut through re-engineering. Volkswagen has a thirty-hour work week, France is adopting a thirty-three-hour week, and Japan is aiming to shorten its workweek from 44 to 40 hours (Rifkin, 1995).

Second, we must develop The Third Sector

To solve the problem of the millions of unemployed Brits whose plight is making politicians and police alike uneasy, Rifkin says we've got to look to the 350,000 non-profit organisations in the UK that deal in social services, health care, education, research, the arts, religion, advocacy, etc. to absorb the labour and talent of men and women no longer needed in the market and government sectors. The independent sector, the volunteer sector, the Third Sector, the non-profit sector, they're all the same thing. In the Third Sector people who hold jobs in the market and government sectors join hands in their off hours (made possible by the shorter workweek) with the not-employed, basically, to revitalize their communities (Rifkin, 1996).

Third, get everyone back in school

Charles Handy thinks we all should be given three years of lifetime educational credit vouchers to be cashed in at any university or college that will accept us. So, in addition to everyone engaging in community good works, the unemployment problem would also be tackled by everyone having access to higher education, whenever the spirit moved them. Handy questions whether eighteen is the right age to decide whether or not to do more formal education, and in what. Why not any age? We might also ask, why only three years worth of education? A modest proposal might be six years. That's how long it takes to do a BA at the OU.

———————

Pilot Peter Bolton in the next chapter asked himself when he turned fifty, do I really want to get up at 4:15 and get home at midnight til I'm sixty, or until I fall over? The answer was no and with his OU science degree and flying experience, he will be one of those part-time, consulting professionals around the edge of the airline industry, for many years beyond sixty.

Chapter 16

Peter Bolton, Who Studied at the Gatwick Hilton

The main obstacles to surmount are mental. Am I clever enough? Do I have the determination? Especially when you are two weeks behind and the assignment takes far longer to complete than you expect. Silly hiccups such as trying to write a Pascal program in a hotel in Miami without a PC on the day the assignment is due. Or sitting in a hotel room in Manchester and getting to the bit where it says `View the video now before continuing,' with no video tape and no video recorder. I can't really imagine you tearing out to the Middle East, microphone in hand to interview me, but I wish you the best of luck with your project.

This was Peter's written response to my request that he take part in this book. We did, however, manage to meet up at his home in Luton on one of his rare visits to England from his new job with Saudi Arabian Airlines.

Peter, graying, medium height, hazel eyes, informal blue jacket and tan trousers, told me he was born in Dunoon 1944. His father, an electrical engineer for the Royal Navy, was a Canadian citizen and shortly after taking his family over to Canada, was killed in an accident when Peter was five. Peter was then raised in England where his mother remarried. He left school at eighteen with two A-levels and flew transport aircraft for the RAF for twelve years. Then he flew the B737, B767, and B757 for Britannia Airways for eighteen years. He left in April 1994 under a redundancy scheme and got a two-year contract as an A300 Airbus captain for the Saudis. He started the OU in 1988, taking mainly science subjects. He is married and has two daughters at university, while his wife, Diane, a secretary, is in her fifth year towards an OU degree. Peter would like to continue and get an honours degree.

Your reasons for doing a university degree?

The main reason was, I never went to university when I was a kid. The grades I got at A-level weren't good enough to get me in, so I joined the air force, which is a sausage machine where young men go in one end and pilots come out the other end, and you're so busy that it's not til years later you think, Gee, I wish I had gone to University.

Another reason is that one of the problems in my game is you may lose your licence, which depends on all sorts of things, ratings, training, base checks, and the medical. We have a medical every six months. And if I failed it, I had no other qualifications. And the third reason was the fact that we spend an awful lot of time in hotel rooms, the Gatwick Hilton, you name it, we've been there. You spend too much time in bars and watching TV and I thought I could do something more useful with my time.

Also, I wanted to do something new. I had tried to be a trainer in Britannia. You apply and your name is then circulated amongst the current trainers, and they vote, and three times I tried to be a trainer on the 737 and they said, Sorry, you didn't get enough votes. So I asked myself, what else can I do? I'd become a bit of a mouse in a treadmill.

Any other obstacles besides those of trying to study abroad?

My early education was marked by a lot of change, a lot of moving around. I changed schools every two or three years. My stepfather was an architect and to get promoted you had to keep moving, especially in local government. I remember passing the eleven plus and getting settled into grammar school and then we moved. And the subjects which were available depended on the local examining board, so I was always saying, Well, now I can't do this, I'll have to do that. I've always struggled with chemistry because I had to go to evening classes to study it and that teacher got sick, so we studied on our own, and I failed the chemistry exam.

When I first started the OU, Diane and I had one or two squabbles because I'd come home and disappear up into my kennel and get on with an assignment that was due, and she'd say, You're only home three days and I don't see anything of you. But once she started doing it herself, she understood what I've been going through. So now I'm worried about this move to Saudi Arabia and what to do with the house and the dog, and she's worried about her course work.

How have your studies changed you?

What it's done for me is I've met a lot of different people that have nothing to do with aviation, whatsoever. I've mucked in with them and enjoyed their company. Getting on with people out in the field for the geology or in the lab for the chemistry and physics. When you start talking about what's your job, I try to avoid that question because I don't want to talk about what I do, I want to learn what other people do. It's broadened my outlook on education, life, and people, getting to know women having to run families on their own, blokes struggling with different problems.

You see it is possible to change. You say, I can afford to take the risk. Having achieved that degree has given me the basic self-confidence to change. Flying is like a game of golf. You're as good as your last shot. You've got to keep looking at your performances. You've got to be self-critical, you need to suffer from a little bit of under-confidence because there's nothing worse than being over-confident. You've got to internalize your performance and say to yourself, How's it going? Is the approach working out as it should do? Am I doing it right, all the time?

Working with those different people affected my on-the-job relationships as well. When I first got promoted, there were a lot of people coming up behind me for their commands and they'd ask, What problems did you have? What happened to you? Because a captain is assessed as an overall package. They've got parameters they can apply to your flying skills, but you're also judged as a manager of a team. And towards the end of flying the 737 I flew with a lot of young guys. Remembering the problems you had when you were new on the airplane, you knew what mistakes they were going to make. But you have to let them work it out for themselves because they'll remember it better.

What's been the impact of your studies on your career?

I've been able to take a major step and give up a job that wasn't suiting me. I've taken a big gamble moving to this other company, because I may or may not be successful. If Diane can come out, then we'll do it. But if it doesn't work out, I won't be hanging on for the be all and end all. Luckily I've got a decent pension scheme in the background that gives me flexibility.

When I consulted Diane about the decision, she was very concerned about the money side of things. No more pay coming in and would I get another job? Wasn't fifty too young to retire? She was as worried as I was about what might go wrong. But the degree gave me the flexibility to say, I don't need to work and I can stop if she doesn't want to come out and join me in Jeddah. The plan at the moment is for her to come out towards the end of next month for a three-week visit, with her new course books to keep her company, and meet some of the people I've met and try to find her feet out there.

What's the most important use you make of your degree?

The course itself taught me how to learn in a different way and with this very intensive course to learn the Airbus, I've been using the same techniques I used studying for my degree. A lot of repetition, drawing diagrams, writing things out, different methods for memorizing things. Both my reading and memory skills are better than they used to be. I have to read standing up in my room because some of the stuff is so damned boring. Our manuals were written by the French and translated into English by a German. So you can imagine what the sentences are like.

Saudi pilots and we, the Qajis, learn the material differently, and the system is designed for them and we have to cope with it. They memorize the Koran from a very early age so they have very good recall memories. In the cockpit they will go through routines very quickly because they learnt it all by heart. The switchery you have to do in a specific order. We, on the other hand, are constantly asking ourselves, What am I doing next? Why am I doing it? Because there are things that aren't in the book. When there is no yellow line to follow, what do you do? Work it back to first principles. You've got to think flexibly. That's the only way round it.

How has continuing your education changed your ideas about work?

I'm not afraid of the future. I've got something to sell now. I've got an education, a degree, years of airline experience, so I can always look for a job around the edge of the airline industry. I will always be in aviation but I haven't worked out how. There are so many things I could do. Diane, on the other hand, is aiming for a dramatic career change. She has a specific target, public health, whereas I'm a bit of a dreamer, rather than being somebody who says, this is where I'm going. I'm not saying I'm totally lost at the moment, but I'm milling around a bit. Right now, my target is to get my star and survive at Saudi, but beyond that, I'm not looking any further than the two-year contract.

One of the problems with being with a company for eighteen years is you really do get in a rut. You can't see anything beyond your next Tenerife, your next Paphos. All of a sudden, I've deliberately pulled myself out. I've said, I want to find something else to do. The Middle East perhaps is a short-term thing until I have worked out what it is.

How did your studies affect your interests?

I got more into computing as a result of the computer course, so it reinforced an interest that I had. The language they used on that course was Pascal so I bought Pascal subsequently. Thus far I use it mostly for spreadsheets, keeping my flying hours up to date, keeping track of my expenses. What I'm really interested in is working with the NASA Voyager spacecraft images, which I got from a friend at NASA. One of the last chapters in a course in geology had to do with the outer planets and satellites. And the NASA images I've got are the same ones used in the book delving into how these tiny little satellites are formed. I've got it all on CD Rom and they give you a small program which allows you to display them on the screen. And I've got a copy of the original images that spacecraft took, not cooked, not warmed, not messed around in any way. It's a case of having the time to go through them, I'd like to change the routines to suit me, if I were clever enough. One of the very first ones I tried turned out to be Saturn with its rings and I was awestruck by this.

I've always been interested in photography and given the chance, I'd like to do what a friend has done. He's a brilliant cameraman and he's been down in Antarctica with David Attenborough doing *Life in the Freezer* and you can tell his voice, there's only one Scots there doing the underwater work. But that would be fascinating to do, with my scientific background, and doing imagery and photography with it. I've got a film here I made for Diane to show her what goes on in Jeddah, the houses, souks, the roads.

What was most important in your life before and after your degree?

Before, my career was always the most important thing, and the family tagged along. I don't know if it's a coincidence that I left my last company at the same time as I completed my degree. Perhaps it has made me more long-term in my thinking, asking, why am I doing this? In my last two years with the company I was working out of Manchester airport, commuting from here to a little room up in Manchester because we weren't able to sell the house. It made me sit back and think, do I really want to do this til I'm sixty or until I fall over, whichever comes first? I've done days where I left here at 4:15, worked a twelve-hour day, and driven back and got home at midnight. I can do it but it certainly isn't something you want to do a lot.

And now, after, my family is more important to me. A man thinks of himself as a provider for the family. To be successful, you provide for your family better. Now that my kids are grown up, money's no longer a problem and you think, I've spent all my time worrying about my career, but is it that important if you've got no family to come home to? There are so many people in this game on their second and third marriages. A lot of it has to do with being away, but also to achieve the standards required, when you do come home you have to get out the books.

Why would you recommend continuing education to other men?

For the sense of achievement that I experienced. I got to the end of the course and went up and shook the Vice-Chancellor by the hand in front of my family and everybody else. It was very much a family day with a lot of older people. The lady who got the biggest cheer of the day had got to be eighty. It was a totally different atmosphere from my daughter's graduation. The Vice-Chancellor made the families cheer for the graduates and then he made the graduates clap hands for the families that supported them. And he said something to every one of us. Thank you for supporting the Open University, he said to me.

It can also have a good effect on your family. Not only is Diane doing a degree, but my elder daughter, who failed her first year of university and got married, said if my old father can do it, I can, and she's now at Middlesex University doing a course for probation officers. And she'll become a full probation officer rather than an assistant. And the younger will get her PhD in biology this June.

I recommend it all the time. My colleagues ask me about my studies, even guys who've got degrees, because they don't use them, they're not relevant to work. And they're equally bored with what they're doing. Once you know the airplane, the mechanics, the systems, the procedures, it's difficult to go back and read those books again and again and again. People still have the interests they had at university, so they've come to me and said, How do you get on? How do you cope with it?

I know you concentrated in the sciences, but I'm wondering what you consider the most serious social or economic problem today in the UK.

The problem that worries me most is Mrs. Thatcher's Gimme society, grab for yourself society. There's not a lot of caring going on. You get what you can for yourself, and never mind your neighbour. The cutbacks on public services, cutbacks in hospital treatment mean that old folks are dying of cold in their own homes. Obviously, nobody's looking after them. Nobody's popping in saying, are you all right? These old folks are the people who were fighting during the Second World War and that's why we're here talking English instead of German. These people gave their time and efforts and we benefited from them. The hardened social side of the country is my biggest worry.

`Gift work' is done for free for charities and non-profits, for neighbours and the community. In the Second Age, the age of working, Peter organised an employees' social club at Manchester airport. As he edges toward the Third Age, the age of living, why not an oldies' social club somewhere in the world, somewhere on the edge of the airline industry?

Chapter 17

Education As The Answer

Education should never have been allowed to become something that has a definite beginning and a definite end. The very concept of `returning' should not be one we recognize because education itself should be ongoing, without beginning or end.... Is it really hopelessly utopian to suggest that education and life itself should be woven indelibly together? Difficult, yes, difficult to grapple with because it is a simple idea and the simple idea is most often the most profound, and radical. Difficult, then, but not impossible, as the many eloquent voices in this book testify (Russell, 1991, p.viii).

A lot of smart people agree with Willy Russell. Charles Handy says, `When education becomes an essential investment, whether as a passport to a core job or as a route to acquiring a saleable skill on the outside, then to ration it is absurd. It is equally absurd to try to shove it all in at the beginning of life, or to think that it can all happen in classrooms, or to ration it later on to those who were cleverest at 18 years of age. A new world of work requires upside-down thinking in education (p.138).'

The only expandable space left

As he was getting acquainted with his new post as Vice-Chancellor of the OU, Sir John Daniel (1991) gave a talk in which he deplored the disappearance of the ozone layer, arable land, old forests, and pure water from the earth as the population swells from 3 billion when the OU was founded to 6 billion in the year 2000. The only space left where there is room for growth in today's world, he said, is intellectual space. The OU is, naturally, Sir John's idea of the ideal form of offering individuals around the globe the opportunity to expand their personal intellectual territory. Its hallmarks are insisting that (1) degree-level knowledge be accessible to all, and (2) mastery of knowledge is demonstrated at exit—more than other universities do.

A radical agenda

Paddy Ashdown (1996), leader of the Liberal Democrats, says that if he had been subjected to selection in his schooling, he would have failed at eleven and left at fourteen. He says our three crucial educational needs are improving pre-school education from age three, recognising the importance of the information revolution, and, creating a `framework for lifelong learning in which everyone is guaranteed a period of education or training at a time of their choice in adult life.' He is talking a radical agenda here and it's going to cost money.

Smart adults flocking to colleges and universities

Record numbers of students, full- and part-time, are enrolling in further education colleges. `Conscious of their need for new skills and better qualifications, people are beating a path to their local colleges and in many cases making considerable sacrifices to pay the fees.' They have to. Employers will send workers on short courses to meet specific company objectives, like learning new safety regulations, but many are too short-sighted to support employees who want to earn NVQs. Yet the Government's far-sighted `Lifetime Learning' goals for the country are 50 per cent of the workforce studying for NVQs by 1996, and 50 per cent qualified to at least NVQ3, craft level, by the year 2000 (MacLeod, 1994b). If it happens, Big Business and the Government won't be responsible. You'll be.

Ironically, the chance of getting a company to pay for your schooling is better the more education you already have. In 1994, twenty-six per cent of graduate employees received in-work training in the previous month, compared with 18 per cent of employees with A-levels, 13 per cent of people with GCSEs, and 4 per cent of those with no qualifications. The highly-educated also got the greatest financial return from their courses. `Going to university doesn't just mean a one-off boost to your earning power. It also confers access to further training and education throughout your life.... (Cooper, 1996).'

If part-timers are included, mature students are the majority in higher education. More mature students entered HE in 1990 than young students and the gap's increasing. Further, research by the Council for National Academic Awards found that mature students up to the age of 40 with few or no formal qualifications are the best performers (Kingston, 1994). A finding confirmed at Plymouth University. Here mature students aged 25 and over who enter with nontraditional qualifications are getting significantly better degrees than younger students who enter with A-levels. Among 7,000 students graduating between 1991 and 1995 mature students were clearly superior to those aged 21-25, who in turn outperformed the 18-20-year-olds (Hunt, 1995).

Graduates say they benefited on the job

Three-quarters of Open University graduates surveyed from 1975 to 1984 said they had enjoyed occupational changes as a result of their studies. Forty-eight per cent said their pay went up and 63 per cent of them said their new qualifications were crucial to that increase. Forty per cent got promoted, with 62 per cent saying their new qualifications were responsible. Seventeen per cent found a whole new occupation for which 70 per cent said their degrees were essential. Other positive changes were moving to a more specialist job within their occupation, moving up to managerial status, and moving to a new organisation. In these moves, their studies had made the difference for 61 per cent or more (Woodley, 1988).

Learning, another word for changing

`Change, however, does not have to be forced on us by crisis and calamity. We can do it for ourselves. If changing is...only another word for learning, then the theories of learning will also be theories of changing. Those who are always learning are those who can ride the waves of change and who see a changing world as full of opportunities not damages. They are the ones most likely to be the survivors in a time of discontinuity. They are also the enthusiasts and the architects of new ways and forms and ideas. If you want to change, try learning one might say, or more precisely, if you want to be in control of your change, take learning more seriously (Handy, p.44).'

Tony Osmond, whom you'll meet next, regrets not getting a degree in music in the First Age. But, however late, his degree sets him up beautifully for success in the Third Age in work that can never be fully automated, gardening, and in a host of gift work activities.

Chapter 18

Tony Osmond, Totally Calmed Down

I would have liked to do some teaching, but I'm too old to take the teaching certificate. The age limit is 55. The wages aren't very good to start with, but they're increasing all the time. And in addition to ordinary teaching, there is the administrative side of it, night school work, lots of opportunities. Men have as much right to nontraditional jobs as women. What's to stop us? Heavy engineering's going, shipbuilding's going, the steel industry. Men have got to take service jobs.

James Anthony Osmond, or Tony as he likes to be called, was born in 1936 and was raised by his auntie and grandmother in Wigan. He left school with one O-level and trained in telecommunications with the City and Guilds. He began the OU in 1982 and got his BA in 1992. He lives in Southampton with his second wife, Susan, also an OU graduate. Since 1989 he has worked full-time as a gardener, having retired voluntarily after three decades as a British Telecom engineer. He is eager to next complete either a BSc honours degree or a diploma in Health and Social Welfare. Tony is short, fit, balding, blue-eyed, and turned up for his interview on the campus of the University of Southampton in jeans and a smart blue jumper.

Your reasons for doing a university degree?

I have three educated children so I thought I'd better do something to get up there with them. I had a workmate who'd started the previous year and he'd gone to summer school and he said it was brilliant. There was so much turmoil in my life at the time. I did it on the spur of the moment. I started with the technology and science foundation courses. At first I was just dribbling down the field in no apparent direction. And it wasn't til I remarried that the goalposts came into view.

What obstacles did you have?

My first wife thought it was a waste of time and money. It was the same when I started the clarinet. She was dead set against it and she'd say, You and that bloody flute! So my only obstacle was lack of backup and encouragement. It showed itself in several failures because I didn't study properly. Instead of getting down to it, I'd watch television. My problems really started when I went to the second level. If you apply the same effort to second-level courses you applied on the first, it doesn't work. I found out to my cost you can't dawdle along.

But with a new wife since '88, she motivated me, and I sailed through the rest of the courses. I was also motivated by my mother's increasing age. She was eighty this year. After my father was killed in the war, she remarried an American and has lived in Florida ever since. But it's she who's paid my university bills all the way through, including six summer schools. My mother flew over from the States for the degree ceremony in 1993 in the Southampton Guild Hall.

I didn't actually fail the eleven-plus. I got equal marks with the person who got the one place, he was the son of a teacher. The headmaster was up in arms about it because I should have got that one place. Money was scarce in those days, they didn't have technical colleges as they have now, so once you `failed' the 11-plus, that was it. When I went into the Army in 1954, I had the choice of cook or medical orderly. Those were the two options in the army for an enlisted man. If you had only a little education, say a couple of GCEs, they'd put you in the RAF. If you had three or four GCEs, you were likely to end up with a real commission.

One of the things I didn't learn, which is a real obstacle, is advanced maths. You didn't learn things like algebra unless you went to grammar school. Now, even today, when I see an algebraic formula, my mind goes completely blank. When I was doing the science foundation course, I had a private tutor for maths for six months. Even at the end of that, I was no wiser. I can't do a simultaneous equation or a quadratic, or simplify a simple algebraic equation, because I never learnt it. But if you give me ordinary mathematics, I can calculate fine.

How have your studies changed you?

The changes are due really to a combination of my studies and my second wife. I met her at Durham University summer school in 1986. We were both doing geology. Then over that year working with BT enabled me to keep in touch over the phone. And the next July, ten days before my 25th wedding anniversary with my first wife, my first wife moved out and my second wife moved in. I took this seven-ton truck from Wigan down to Romsey and loaded up Susan's stuff with her husband looking on. It was a funny day, that. I left British Telecoms in 1987 and we got married in April 1988.

I have a reputation as a know-all with my workmates. If there's an answer to be made, they'll say, Oh, oh, we're going to have a lecture. I know a little about a lot, because my degree is made up of all sorts of courses with geology the main one. I enjoyed everything, Health and Disease, Third World Studies. What I've mainly gained is knowledge. I must have written fifty essays, 2,000 words each one including a 10,000-word project on Highways and Byways.

The other thing that's come out of it is, I used to be easily ruffled. I used to argue a lot with mates at British Telecom. I had the habit of opening my mouth before putting my brain in gear. To the detriment of many relationships. But since coming on this job, I can truthfully say I have never lost my temper with any workmate. Somehow I have totally calmed down. You can't get overstressed when you're studying, because otherwise knowledge goes out a fast as it comes in. My new wife has a diploma in education. She's a string instrument player, a peripatetic, she teaches violin and viola, and she needed a degree to go up the pay scale. She got her degree two years before I did and went straight to the top of the scale. Anyway, she made out schedules for my study and that enabled me to pass the courses. She gave me 100 per cent backing and I never failed again.

What's been the impact of your studies on your career?

I wish I'd got my degree when I was ten years younger. I could have got my PGCE then and I would have gone into teaching, something I wanted very much to do. Gardening's a job, like BT which was a job, full-stop. I've never really been satisfied in any job I've done. If I'd have got this degree as a youngster, I'd have gone either into the merchant navy, or into music. Either one would have made a fine career.

What's the most important use you make of your degree?

In speaking. I use the telephone a lot, to ring publishers to hire music. All orchestras do that. It costs a fortune to buy a piece of music. So when the orchestra wants a certain piece of music, I've got to find out who publishes it. Take our next concert. I needed three pieces of music. *Don Juan* by Strauss, Brahms *Symphony No. 1*, and Tchaikovski's *Romeo and Juliet*. Tchaikovski and the Brahms, no problem. I go to the main publisher which is Concord. They are the main suppliers of those particular composers. But when it comes to the Strauss, I had to do some research. The original publishers had sold that piece to a publisher called C. F. Peters in 1931. And any publisher does not hold the entire works of a given composer. I might end ringing up a publisher in Germany.

How has continuing your education changed your ideas about work?

I knew from the beginning that no matter what subjects I studied, it wouldn't make any difference to my work with BT. Because if your face doesn't fit, you'll not get on. Promotion is dependent on your first line supervisor's liking of you, and if he doesn't like you, he will not put your name forward for promotion, no matter what qualifications you have. Unfortunately, quite often, I didn't get on with my peers.

As for my early retirement, I was lucky. I came away with thirty-three years, a little lump sum and quite a good pension. BT's got rid of thousands of men, a lot of them with less than ten years service. With less than ten years service, your pension is pathetic. If you're in your forties, you have no chance of getting another job. The march of technology is doing away with labour. You can't hold back technology. So, all a man can do, really, is make sure he's got all the qualifications he can. And go into a field that is expanding, not reducing labour. The only way to a job today is to have as many qualifications as possible.

I also think men should change their ideas about what's appropriate. I've got a friend whose son just got his doctorate from Oxford. He's a mathematician. And he got invited to look round one of those city analyst places, to work in the stock market as a mathematician. And he found it very interesting, so he's been sidetracked. As a mathematician, he always thought he'd be an academic. There are all sorts of jobs out there that people don't think about.

How did your studies affect your interests?

Again, my interests are very much bound up with my second wife. I'm into music, a lot. I help to run one of the main school orchestras in Hampshire. It's a feeder orchestra for the two main orchestras in this shire. Also I'm the librarian to the City of Southampton symphony orchestra which is a very nice job. My wife plays the violin in that orchestra.

I've always been very active. We're both avid walkers and when we lived in Wigan we used to go up to the Lake District regularly. We belong to the Open University Geological Society and this University's Geological Society. So we do a fair amount of walking and six months ago on a Saturday just like this, windy, the rain coming vertically down, we spent the day in a claypit doing a geology fieldtrip. How this clay was got out, how it was mixed, graded for different things like ceramics, pots, electrical insulators.

And it's only since I remarried that I did a tour of between three and four thousand miles in France. I never went anywhere like that before. And since I came down here, I have learned to sail. I have my own yacht, a 20-footer, on the River Itchen on a pontoon.

I keep saying I'll go back to York, it was my favorite summer school, to volunteer. I belong to the Association of Graduates and every year they ask if anybody would like to come to summer school to help with the disabled. They're always asking for invigilators as well. It would be nice to go back to summer school. They're nice people there.

What was most important in your life before and after the degree?

Before, my children were the most important. It's only the fact that I had children and wasn't going to leave them while they were still in their formative years that I stayed with the wife until the youngest turned eighteen and they'd all gone to college. Most important now is my life with the second wife. It's a proper marriage of intellectual equals. We greet each other when we come in with a kiss and we like to cuddle.

Why would you recommend continuing education to other men?

It focuses your mind. You either focus or fail. And if you don't have a goal, you've got to find one, and then if you have determination, you'll get that goal. I would say a degree from an ordinary university is a very easy way to get a degree. The length of time those students spend per term actually working, put that against a full six credits of studying on your own and there's no comparison whatsoever. A lot of business people look upon a person who's doing a postal degree as somebody's who is totally reliant. Because they know they've had to study hard to do a postal degree. It's a hell of a hard job.

It makes you a lot more self-confident. I can hold my own now in any scientific discussion, especially in geology. I know exactly what we're talking about, anticlines, inclines, different strata, what a moraine is or a flashflood. Before I was actually quite shy. Now at the end of the term for the school orchestra, I can go out there and give a speech. I can talk to two to three hundred parents, and say let's give a vote of thanks to the orchestra, I hope they've all enjoyed it, and we're losing thirty of our children now to other orchestras and thirty more are coming in. Let's have a big hand of applause for the conductor. This is something I never could have done fifteen years ago, before I started my studies.

Tony is, I'm sure, a very good gardener, but wouldn't it be nice if the age restrictions on teachers were torn up so that the shortages could be alleviated? Particularly the current shortage in craft, design, and technology classes, by men like Tony (see Chapter 25)?

Chapter 19

Future Job Security

> The third-sector vision offers a much-needed antidote to the materialism that has so dominated twentieth-century industrial thinking. While work in the private sector is motivated by material gain, and security is viewed in terms of increased consumption, third-sector participation is motivated by service to others and security is viewed in terms of strengthened personal relationships and a sense of grounding in the larger earth community (Rifkin, p.246).

How many workers have job security?

Charles Handy talks about twenty/eighty organisations. They are so named because 80 per cent of the value of a company's products or services is contributed by people *not* in the organisation. Similarly, 20/80 can refer to the fact that only 20 per cent of workers in a given country, Japan being one, have the security of lifetime employment because they're in the central cores of large organisations. The other 80 per cent are on the outside, contract workers and part-time, temporary workers with quite limited job security.

Will Hutton talks about job security a little differently. You remember his 30/30/40 society of Chapter 15. It identified as enormously insecure the 30 per cent of the working population which isn't working. Then there is the 30 per cent whose part-time, casual work makes them marginalised and insecure. Well, the fact is, the last 40 per cent category considered `privileged' includes self-employed people who have held their jobs for only two years and part-timers whose jobs have lasted only five years. The 40 category also includes the thirty-five per cent of full-time employees who earn less than 80 per cent of the median wage. So, it is more like 20 to 30 per cent of British workers who have anything vaguely resembling our old notions of job security.

Another twist is that the elite core isn't going to find security the old way, by moving up the hierarchy. Vertical chains of command are giving way to horizontal structures where people work in teams pooling their skills. In this new kind of organisation, security rests on one's reputation as a good team member and on making as many moves as possible across the organisation (McRae, 1996).

`Job security' is a thing of the past. What we now have is `employment security'. The individual must build his own security by putting ever more skills in his portfolio, continuing to learn, accepting part-time and freelance jobs, and only selecting employers who will add value to his career. Women are much better at this game than men; women retrain faster, they jump at part-time and temporary employment, and they take only three months to find a job while the average man takes five (MacErlean, 1996).

The work ethic of Generation X

Interviews with over a thousand higher-educated young people in North America and Europe revealed that the young don't believe employment is guaranteed either by benevolent employers or by progressive governments. So the young are not going after fixed jobs. They are looking for project-based work where they can use their brains and are in control of their time. They want projects that provide variety, build expertise, and increase marketable, transferable skills. Their definition of employment security is total self-reliance.

Generation X distinguishes between winner and loser employers. Winners are super modern. These organisaations have visible female and ethnic minority employees in senior posts. They have working conditions that are flexible and life-friendly. They are at ease with new technologies. The loser organisation is full of gray-suited, middle-aged men who don't know how to type.

This new, security-in-the-self ethic is the prerogative of only the top quarter of the population, those with higher education. But if you are in that top quarter, if you've got that degree, who says you have to be of Generation X? Wrinklies with degrees have the added advantage of years of experience and being retrained (Wilkinson, 1994).

And after the Third Industrial Revolution?

Jeremy Rifkin says in the future most people won't find their identities in paid work anyway. So, eventually `employment security' will also lose its meaning. Everyone, regardless of which 30/30/40 category one is in, will find identity in community service. If a man has no paid employment (not one of the rare, privileged core elite), he will be supported by an adequate social wage from the government, but not welfare payments and benefits as we know them. However, this social wage will have nothing to do with how `productive' he is working in the Third Sector.

As Rifkin puts it, `Unlike the market economy, which is based solely on "productivity" and therefore amenable to the substitution of machines for human input, the social economy is centered on human relationships, on feelings of intimacy, on companionship, fraternal bonds, and stewardship-- qualities not easily reducible to or replaceable by machines. Because it is the one realm that machines cannot fully penetrate or subsume, it will be by necessity the refuge where displaced workers of the Third Industrial Revolution will go to find renewed meaning and purpose in life....(pp.291-292).'

In Chapter 20, Raj Ragiwala's applied computing degree, combined with seventeen years' work experience, give him, for the present, employment security and typical Generation X confidence in himself. But Raj also has an edge on Rifkin's futuristic idea of identity based in service to one's community—he belongs to a community called Darji.

Chapter 20

Rajesh Ragiwala, Who Gave Up Cricket

BT's got very few job sharers or part-time workers. Primarily what they do is get rid of employees and contract the work out. For example, we used to have our own catering staff. They sold the whole lot and gave a contract to the Trusthouse Forte Group. The catering employees who used to work for BT moved to this new company. Currently, the people who transfer BT employees from one building to another are an internal estates group and BT's looking to sell that to the outside. My group does long-term forecasting. In five years they could decide, We can get some company to do the same for us. If they say, You're out next month, then you take your skills and see what you can do with them.

I remembered Dial House in Central London from when we first moved here. I spent many an afternoon in the long queue of customers on the ground floor trying to get our phone connected. Back then you had contact with real people, but with chaps like handsome Raj in his smart black blazer and purple tie on the upper floors managing things, BT's inefficiencies of yesteryear have shrunk, along with its workforce.

Rajesh, 38, was born in Uganda into a Hindu family that had immigrated from India. They came to London when Raj was nine and he went to school in Harrow, earning six O-levels and two A-levels. He began the OU in 1983 and finished an honours BA in 1994. He is married and currently studying French in evening classes with his wife of ten years, Rekha. He was promoted during his studies from a BT clerical officer to commercial officer in which job he also performs middle management functions several weeks in the year when his supervisor is on holiday.

Your reasons for doing a university degree?

There were two reasons. One was to progress in employment. My very first job was with BT, I've been with them seventeen years. And when a vacancy gets announced, out of 150,000 people working, four to five hundred may apply for that job and they have to shortlist from that number to interview about four people. The only way they can do it is by looking at qualifications, then experience, so with a degree, you have more chance of making the shortlist. The second reason was I didn't really have the opportunity to go to university when I finished my A-levels. It was the normal thing in my family to start working fairly early and there was no incentive to carry on studying.

On the other hand, it was my Dad who wrote off for the original OU package. He said, this might be good for you. Why don't you do this? You should have been a scholar. After he retired from the civil service here, he went on to do homeopathy. He passed the qualification, got a licence and insurance. He's always been quite keen to study.

What obstacles did you have?

The family expectation that I go out and work at an early age and start earning money. I would have liked to carry on and finish my studies because it is far easier simply studying than working and studying. In terms of my courses, I didn't benefit from the tutorials. I was always too far ahead or too far behind, so after I started my second course I only went to a couple tutorials and then decided I could better use that time. I was more of a loner than a lot of students, although I'm not a loner otherwise.

Because my work involved going out, as well as being in the office, I managed to rush around and get my BT outside work done in the morning and then study for two or three hours when I was still fresh and could concentrate. Then after my studies, I'd finish my BT office work.

How have your studies changed you?

When I joined BT, everything was new and I had lots of things to learn, different places to go to work. But after I got into the job, I found myself vegetating. It was like picking up your toothbrush in the morning and brushing your teeth. I thought there's got to more to work than this. The language within the company is so narrow, we use all these abbreviations, and the people I talked to were all other company people. Once I started my studies, my mind opened up to this whole new world outside BT.

The courses are designed to make you question more than you ordinarily do. In all fields, not just at work, I'm more critical. I look at a building, how did they manage to get that up? How does it stay up? I look at a small piece of work and ask, how can we make this better? Or a way of doing something, is it the best way to go about this? It happened right away with my first course in technology, this completely new perspective. I don't take anything for granted. I turn it around, upside down, sideways, and start thinking in lateral terms. They drum it into you over and over in the texts, is this the only way to look at something?

What's been the impact of your studies on your career?

My courses were work-related and had to do with computing. They make me more marketable if I have to leave the company. I would have liked to use the degree to progress up the line, but BT has been reducing staff for the past five years. They have lost over 100,000 people in that time and also the grade that I want to move into in management has been shrinking every year.

But my studies did make a big difference when I moved from clerical officer to commercial officer. In the interview everything changed totally when I mentioned my studies. They were so interested. The interview lasts thirty minutes and I spent twenty minutes telling them all about the OU and what I'd gained from it. It seemed like a different world to them. I think when they discussed the interviews they remembered me because I had told them something fresh and that's why I got the promotion. My commercial officer grade was originally a sales job, but the work I do now is long-term planning and forecasting. And some subjects like data models and data bases have been very useful in my present work.

What's the most important use you make of your degree?

If I put down something on paper before, it might fill a whole A4 size sheet, whereas now I could summarize that page in five or six lines. I know exactly what I want to say. Same in talking. If I have to give a presentation, I put down my objectives. I concentrate on what is the most important information and present it so people get it immediately. When I'm doing my manager's work there's a lot of information to put over at our team meeting which we have once a month. I use it when I do courses internally and have to make presentations. And once a quarter we have a big meeting of four or five hundred people. I'll put my hand up now and ask questions in front of the people, whereas before I didn't have the confidence.

What are your educational plans?

I've always thought I'd use the degree as a stepping stone to further education. I might go on to do an MBA. BT might even sponsor me, once they come out of reducing numbers and get back to normality.

My going on in school made my whole family realize that once you're through college, it's not the end of your study days. You can still progress and get qualifications. My wife is now thinking of taking a BTec at the college because her work is changing into information technology. And we're studying

French because a lot of jobs advertised say a working knowledge of French would be useful.

What was most important in your life before and after the degree?

Before? Sport. I used to do a lot of sport. I used to play cricket for Harrow Cricket Club. I started in the fourth team and made my way to the first team. I was at a very reasonable standard. I used to play Saturday, Sunday, Wednesday, and then I played for BT and they gave me time off to play. I also played in the evening, so all told I played five or six matches a week. And I played football Sunday mornings. But once I started on my degree I had to give up cricket. You start at two o'clock in the afternoon and finish up about eight, then you go into the bar and socialise with the opponents, and you don't get home til 11:30. Also it's expensive. All the equipment and you pay for lunch or tea, and if you got fifty runs or five wickets, you've got to buy everyone a jug of beer. So it worked out to be quite expensive because I used to get a lot of 100s and that's two jugs. My local team, the Green Hill Football Club, we won the league a couple of times, we came runners up twice in the cup. But once I had a home and a mortgage and the expense of studying, I could no longer afford to be so involved in sport.

What is most important now is my wife, my family and my community. Four years ago we bought a bigger house thinking that my parents would move in with us. But they like their independence, they want their own space. Because of the extended family, one son would normally do this. So it's there if they change their minds in the future.

We do two holidays a year, one on our own, and one with the family. Last year, for example, we went to Florida with the family on my wife's side and I hired a coach and drove eleven of us around. And we are part of a community called Darji, Shree Darji Mandal UK. If our family were still in Bombay, my father would be a tailor with a tailoring shop. You've got all these communities related to trades, goldsmiths, locksmiths, shoe menders, builders, farmers, it all goes back to India where you had all these little communities that dealt with that specific trade and they'd pass it down to their children. We've got a community throughout London and the rest of the country and we have various functions throughout the year. And once a year in Luton everyone gets together, three to four thousand people and this is where people meet each other as the start to arranged marriages. I met Rekha at these functions. There are large Darji communities in other countries, Canada, America, so you could meet a partner there as well. When there's an Asian wedding, the whole of that Asian community is invited. We get, on average, a thousand people at a wedding. Big hall, big stage, it's more a social gathering, people chatting away. You wouldn't even know there was a wedding happening on the stage.

A lot of my community, their surname is Tailor. My Dad's name was Tailor back in Bombay. And because his nickname was Ragi, he thought, well, nobody knows me by Tailor, I might as well change my name to Ragiwala. That's where we got our surname. So my father's the first Ragiwala, my older brother's the second, I'm the third, and my younger brother's the fourth. We've got this very small Ragiwala community, the only one in the world, as far as we know.

Why would you recommend continuing education to other men?

In this country there are so many opportunities for people who haven't been able to study in the first place to have a second chance. In countries like India, once you've missed it, there's no way for you to do something on your own time. Here, you've got evening classes, day classes, weekend courses, correspondence study, all you need is the determination to do it. I think mature students do better in their studies because of their experience.

Studying adds a lot to your sense of security at work. It used to be, once you joined BT, you were there for life, like all civil service in this country. Then came the redundancies. However, in spite of them because I've been improving myself constantly, if BT says your last pay packet is next month, I've got something I can take outside and use. It's given me eight courses, eight qualifications if you will, knowledge and experience, so I know I can start again.

You've really got to be flexible in this game. Our organisation changes every six months. Move from one location to another. Learn a new computer package. Don't forget your mobile phone. I've seen managers hide their mobile phones away or leave them at home. They don't want to be associated with the earlier image of people phoning, looking flashy. My attitude is there are all these new technologies coming along. Be flexible, use them.

I got that flexibility from my studies, starting with the technology course. They put up this case where you've got your typical kitchen, cooker there, fridge there, sink there, and they said, we're going to put power, gas, water, all the supplies down here in the middle of the room and everything has to go around it, cooker, fridge, etc. I started rebelling against it straight away. Oooh, I wouldn't want to see it like that, that's crazy. And I had to face the fact that I had real prejudices in my mind about how a kitchen should be laid out, in a square with everything all round. But the idea was to step back and assess the new design on its merits. What are its good points, its bad points? Why was I so anti?

Do you have a traditional household or are you a New Man or a Newish Man?

A Newish Man. We share the cooking and cleaning. I do the Hoovering and make the bed. Put the clothes in the washer. We always go shopping together, do the gardening together. Asian men aren't taught to make any Asian dishes. From an early age the daughters are taught to do the cooking and the sons aren't. I wanted to learn and my wife taught me. There's not enough time in the day for a wife to do all those things. You have to share the work out.

Also, we've shared planning financially for the future. Even if I were paid half as much for a similar job outside BT, I would receive a large compensation for my seventeen years to cushion the blow. And I've been doing various insurances and BT has a share-save scheme I've been doing. Rekha and I have been working together for a long time and saving, so that if one of us loses a job, there's something to fall back on. As long as we can pay back our mortgage we shouldn't have too much trouble.

Raj and Rekha's first use of their French course, incidentally, will not be on the job, but on their next just-the-two-of-us holiday to the South of France.

Chapter 21

More Time for Home Work

> One of the objections from the guys on site was that I was doing all these things for the kids, picking them up and so on, and that wasn't my job. Some people are so rigid, and they can't see any change. One couple we know, the woman still had to do everything, cooking and cleaning— and then staying up till two or three in the morning to study. That is a selfish reaction on the man's part, isn't it? He didn't want to know about looking after the kids or anything. It's short-sighted. You've got to adapt, otherwise you're in a stalemate, and that's no good for anyone, is it? (Pye, 1991, p.226)

What does Charles Handy mean by home work?

Not our traditional notion of school work. That's `study work'. Home work is that whole catalogue of tasks that go on in the home, cooking, cleaning, gardening, caring for children and aging parents, DIY remodeling, shopping. Done willingly or grudgingly, it is all home work.

There's lots of room for improvement here for men. One survey found that 54 per cent of couples say the evening meal should be prepared together, but in 70 per cent of them, the woman did it. Cleaning should be shared equally said 60 per cent of couples, yet cleaning was done mainly by the woman in 68 per cent of these homes. And 36 per cent of couples said washing and ironing should be equally shared, but in 84 per cent of these cases, the woman did it (Sex equality, 1992). And the latest British Social Attitudes Survey found in 79 per cent of households women did the washing and ironing, in 60 per cent women decided what to have for dinner, and in 48 per cent women looked after sick family members alone while men never did so alone (Timmins, 1996a).

In fact, the Mintel Men 2000 survey found that only two per cent of men conform to the New Man image, that is, they do all the household tasks or share them equally with their wives. That's why Mintel came up with the idea of 'Newish Man' who is responsible for just one household task so that a further 18 per cent of men could qualify for this title. (You'll have noted that a much higher percentage of OU men are Newish Men or on their way to being New Men.)

Another indicator that's there's room for improvement here for men is a survey done in 1996 by the Legal and General Insurance Company which found that if Mum had to be replaced (as cook, cleaner, laundress, childminder, nurse, gardener, administrator, odd-job person), it would cost over £16,000 a year. Britain's mothers' 62 hours of home work a week are worth £313 compared with Dad's 23 hours per week worth £117 (Value of a mum, 1996).

A growing task for men, child care

One in five families in Britain is headed by a lone parent and the number of men lone parents is rising steadily. There were 70,000 lone father families in 1970 and 110,000 by 1990. Fifty-year-old Bob Huggins' wife left him six years ago and he has raised their three children singlehanded since. Last year he was made redundant and now cares for them with the money he receives from income support and maintenance. After 33 years of wage work, he decided home work of this kind was more important, but `it is difficult being Mum and Dad 24 hours a day.' He believes `the female side of men comes out a little bit and this is no bad thing' (Harnden, 1994). And 33-year-old Paul Burgoine's wife makes £20,000 a year, much more than he could hope to earn in his career as a nursery officer. So he, too, stays at home to look after their four children. One in five women is now like Paul's wife, the household high earner (Caine, 1996).

Two more tasks set to take off, caring for parents and grandchildren

A 31-year-old north London teacher, Tony Breslin, campaigns to keep open the mental hospital that takes care of his senile father. It is marked for closure, part of the push towards care in the community. If Tony is not successful, he and his 75-year-old mother will be taking care of his dad. Men who reach sixty can expect to live another 19 years, women another 22 years, and somebody's got to take care of them, with residential care running £400 a week (Donegan, 1994).

Then there's the story of Tom and Edna Bramwell who in their fifties began the care of three-year-old Nicky, the child of their daughter who died of leukaemia. More and more grandparents find themselves in the same boat. Age Concerns says grandparents' raising kids is now common practice, due to the pressures of work and rising divorce among parents (Driscoll, 1996).

The National Institute of Health in the States recommends that everyday housework chores, carried out for thirty minutes daily, are as good for the heart as a brisk walk or other vigorous exercise. But among the fifteen men interviewed, only one was getting the full benefit, Eugene MacLaughlin, whom you'll meet next. And the driving force was not health, but guilt for not bringing in an income while getting his law degree. Probably when he's a lawyer, he and Patricia will go back to sharing home work. Except for the cooking.

Chapter 22

Eugene MacLaughlin from Further Education

As far as the role of men in the workplace goes, it's time to get away from what our popular culture expects of us. Studying for a BA, men come to a broader understanding of our role in society. The motivation to study has to come from within the self, but you'll be a better person for it. You'll certainly pick the right wife. You'll definitely have some lively domestic debates.

Eugene was born in Derry, Northern Ireland in 1958, so he is, at age 35, one of the University of North London's more mature law students. He grew up in a Catholic family and both parents were unskilled factory workers. Eugene did nine O-levels and four A-levels at a college of technology and trained at the University of Ulster to be a teacher of business studies. He taught at Ballymoney College of Further Education for six years, starting the OU in 1986. He moved to London in 1990 to teach at a Catholic girls secondary school, and received his honours degree in economics and social science in 1993. He married another teacher, Patricia, less than two years ago, so in addition to all the other changes in his life, Eugene is a newlywed.

We did the interview in a grotty TV lounge with dirty walls and piles of broken furniture at North London's student union. 'Just look at the state of the place,' Eugene kept interjecting with a sigh. He is bearded, wiry, fast-moving, and full of energy and good humour.

Your reasons for doing a university degree?

I had trained as a teacher and was naturally sold on the idea of getting a university degree. And being a business studies/economics person, I could also see there was a financial incentive for studying, anywhere, but the OU could come to me and I could fit my life around it. So I chose it for ease of access.

What obstacles did you have?

Certainly my primary education was quite good. It was a small, rural primary school with some very good teachers, but I was one of those people who `failed' the eleven-plus. I missed school the day it was on. I remember people wanting me to pass. I had an aunt who was a teacher and I remember her giving my mother a book with advice to get me through the eleven-plus. I thought I'd escaped it, but they arranged a resit for me, so I very conveniently had pneumonia when the resit was on. Then I went through secondary school at a time when Northern Ireland was in turmoil, so maybe that has to be held in balance as well.

The thing that has stuck with me is that the expectations of our teachers weren't up to the mark. It's something that I take with me into my own teaching. I would never ever, ever say to anyone, You cannot do something. It's better that they try and fail totally, than for you to have low expectations of people. I literally drifted through St. Brecan's High School. In 1974 I took the further education entrance test which basically meant that if you could read and write, you got a place at the local college of technology. I was very relieved to pass it, so at sixteen I began a vocational business course. That's where I did my O-levels and A-level equivalents. This college was like a half-way house, neither school nor university, but I spent five very good years there, and finished with a higher national diploma in business studies. Then I did teacher training at the University of Ulster.

The high school I went to was reckoned to be the sink school, the place where the failures went. We were policed rather than educated. Maybe we needed policing because there was no one else there to do it. One thing it did put into my head was if you ever lie down and admit defeat, you're screwed. St. Brecan's is in the waterside area of Derry, near a housing estate named Gobnascale, a predominantly nationalist Catholic housing area, which has its fair supply of people doing time for IRA activities, certainly a lot of people I went to school with. If you're reading this, I hope you all get your degrees before you come out, boys!

As for present-day obstacles, tutorials and everything post-foundation tended to be held in Belfast, and that was one hell of a trek on a Saturday. And we all had to come to this side for summer schools.

How have your studies changed you?

As a learner, I'm much more confident. I'm particularly critical of this place, its teaching styles and mode of delivery. I'm a more independent person in my inner, intellectual life. My wife assures me, too, I've got more dogmatic. She's a very political person, she's the thinking, high end of the relationship, while I'm a sort of Ronald Reagan of the relationship. Anyway, our conversations, depending what day of the week it is, tend to degenerate into political debates.

Most of my friends now are females, it's incredible. We're all from the slightly right-wing liberal democratic states of the world. So I've moved away from my social origins in that my father was an active trade union member.

My relationships with women started to change when I traveled to summer school with two women friends. Feminist politics was a whole new ballgame to me. They introduced me to people like Mary Wollstonecraft and Rosa Luxemburg. And the hidden agenda of marriage and how men have exploited women and still are and will continue to do. And how women allow that exploitation.

What's been the impact of your studies on your career?

I always had the idea of doing law at the back of my mind. So having done economics and politics, it was a qualification in its own right. I'm not waving it around, but it's immediately recognizable. The degree does say a lot about people. The idea that you can get on with your own personal study. In my experience as a recruiter, I would give a more sympathetic ear to people who were continuing their education. At the end of the day, that's what life is about, instead of waiting for things to happen.

I knew when I started teaching at Ballymoney, I was not for staying, and that if the option ever came of finding another job and collecting whatever money I could from a redundancy fund, I would do it. There was a reorganisation of further education and they asked for volunteers. So I said, I'm away.

What's the most important use you make of your degree?

It doesn't directly relate to what we're doing here, but I use the analytic-evaluative skills I gained. Sitting down and looking at a particular case, looking at the judgment, taking another approach to that judgment, turning it on its head, arguing completely the opposite. Economics and politics don't fit in much in law at this level, but law in itself is political. Even here, at this university, there are hidden agendas. The biggest hidden agenda in any law course is conformity—You will conform to the laws of society! There's also a hidden agenda of discrimination against black people on this course, although no one would admit it. The school's probably not aware it's there. That is, to be a successful law student and then lawyer you have to hold certain values from the white, middle-class bourgeois.

What are your educational plans?

To finish here and then I'll probably start with the Crown Prosecution Service. Because the local chief crown prosecutor used to be the head teacher in a school I worked in. I imagine I will be working with the CPS for a few years to get the work experience, then I suspect I will end up in private practice of my own. This year of study is for people with university degrees but not in law. After this year we do one more year either to be a solicitor or a barrister. You take the exam at the end of this additional year. Then you've got to work one year for a barrister, and two years for a solicitor. I have sent out 300 applications and to date I haven't found anything. A lot of people don't like going to the Crown Prosecution Service. You're seen as a bit of a pig, working for the oppressive arm of the state. But I have come this far and I know how to survive.

Will I make a good lawyer? Yes. I have a sense of justice. Plus the ability to convince you that all crows are white. Plus self-confidence and a certain arrogance. `My client is innocent, Your Worship, it's another man who is guilty as hell.' Justice is a word that we don't use in this course, but because I'm Irish, I have enough contempt for the English legal system to make it work for me.

How has continuing your education changed your ideas about work?

I confuse other people when I talk about success, because what I have discovered is that success is a peaceful inner life. In 1988 I suffered from a depressive state, and I don't mean feeling down in the dumps, I mean depressive. So if you're happy in what you're doing and you've got a happy married life, and you've got a happy inner life, you've got success.

I had to get help with it, so I was an out-patient at a psychiatric hospital where I got an anti-depressive drug and had nine months of one-to-one therapy. Psychiatry is a bit of a bluff, but the depression passed. My mother and father were splitting up at the time and continually phoning me up, so I think it was reactive more than anything. The cornerstone was basically, you've got to keep active, and say, if I am doing this, I will not allow any intrusion cloud my functioning. And having a long-term educational objective, I could say, Right, I'm going through this, but it will pass. I just kept going on a day-to-day basis. It wasn't very pleasant but it didn't come back.

I had an agenda. I said, What I want is, bum, bum, bum, bum. I want to be in a happy married relationship. I want a bright, cheerful home environment. And if I let people into my life who are going to cause trouble, I'd asked for it.

Success in the short-term is getting through this course. Then, I dare say, success will be becoming a lawyer. That's the vocational area I want to seek success in. Home-wise, success will be getting my wife to remove half the furniture in our house. It's like being married to a jackdaw, it really is.

My ideas about retirement haven't changed. My mother died last year quite young, she was only 59, so I think I have this genetic baggage of cardiovascular illness coming at me somewhere down the line. Having said that, I have always had it in the back of my mind that I will retire from work around my 50th birthday. And I am financially planning for that. As to what I will do with all that free time, I do want to get around a few countries. And you should always be doing something to educate yourself. So perhaps there's a master's or doctorate lurking in there as a retirement project.

I started saving for my retirement when I was twenty-five using a teacher's superannuation scheme. I also bought into an additional voluntary scheme into which I put 15 per cent of my income which supplements my pension contributions. I've been doing that for ten years. So I am going to have one hell of a good, early retirement. My day-to-day finances look like a South American republic, but my long-term finances are absolutely sound, that's just part of me.

How did your studies affect your interests?

They gave me an interest in traveling. One country I want to go to is the United States because in two politics courses we took a look at the US political system. And the Pacific Rim would be interesting economically, certainly by the end of the century, and I'd also like to visit China. I always wanted to visit the Soviet Union but unfortunately it's gone now. That is a tragedy. I didn't travel before coming to London. But now with the proximity of Europe, I have been to Spain, Portugal, France, Luxembourg, the low countries, Germany, Italy. I've tried several times getting to the States, but something has always happened.

Why would you recommend continuing education to other men?

Because it proves to you that you're capable. Staying with it and putting in the time, that sums it up. You've got to say, Right, I'm going to spend 15 to 20 hours a week doing this. I was lucky in that I had the bulk of it over with before I moved and took on a new job. And I was lucky that my wife was in education and we had an unspoken agreement that we would make time for it. Distance learning is a unique form of education, it's unique to the self, because you're very much your own tutor. The lecturing staff here says to us, This is the way it is, because, because, because. In fact, they've noticed that it's the three OU people on this course who are the most critical of their lectures.

Why are men reluctant to take traditional women's jobs?

I'm not. I do the housework. I also do the cooking, for one simple reason—my wife is one hell of a miserable cook. The one thing I detest is the washing up. So when I was living on my own, I ate from paper plates. Housework is no problem. I'm an active person and I like to be doing things. Our only problem is our different personalities. I'm a minimalist. If I have not used something in the last six months, out it goes. For Patricia, who is a technology and art teacher, if it's collectible, it comes into our house. God forbid, if somebody throws something out in our street, I walk ten feet behind her.

Men are quite shocked that I do the housework. The best man at my wedding, he is second generation Irish, a mathematics teacher, and brought up in a very traditional Irish Roman Catholic working class home, and he could not believe it when we invited them round for a meal and it was me that was cooking.

Because of economic circumstances, sometimes there should be a reversal of traditional domestic roles. In times of economic recession there may only be one person working, and if it's the woman, then the only reason I can think of for the man not to be doing the housework, is that he can get away with it. Because I married late in life, I was used to tidying up my own mess, so I didn't come straight out of a domestic situation where the mother role gets transferred to the wife. But, I take this right back to the culture I came from, I felt awfully guilty that first month that Patricia was going to work and I was going to college. I had great difficulty adapting to this course because of traditional ideas.

Do you feel discrimination, coming from Northern Ireland?

I decided a long time ago, when I was an adolescent, that I would eventually leave Northern Ireland. I didn't want to live in a society that I do not agree with. I have very little time for a system that has to bolster itself up the way it does. It never had anything to offer me, and, quite frankly, I didn't have much to offer it.

I don't mind being Paddy, because I recognise myself as being Irish. But the person it really screws up is the Unionist Loyalist Protestant who thinks he is British and he comes over here and discovers, He is Paddy. And that freaks those people out. I would be very insulted if I were regarded as anything other than Irish. As far as discrimination is concerned, I have not seen it. Although I will say, I would not want to be black in this country. I have seen discrimination in the school I worked in, and the area I live in. There is a cultural gulf even between myself and Afro-Caribbeans. I cannot number in my circle of friends, one, single Negro person, although I do have Asian friends. A comparison I would draw between Northern Ireland and England is we have a divided society but at least we have friends in the other community. Here, friendship doesn't seem to exist across that racial gulf, and that's sad and shocking.

––––––––––––––

`Home work' is housework, and as men do less and less paid work, it makes sense for them to spend more time taking care of their homes. But there's only so much to be done about the house. The real place to be putting in more and more hours is what comes next, gift work.

Chapter 23

More Time for Gift Work

We need a new religion to save us, or at least a new fashion. Fraternity, the care for others as much as for oneself, must be our guiding ethic. First learn to love yourself, then your neighbour, but don't forget the neighbour.... It can't be done by laws, or by institutions, or by taxes, for fraternity is one thing that cannot be contracted out or outsourced. It is a core value, and it is established by the example of the people at the core, by the new elites, the fortunate ones (Handy, p.209).

Both Jeremy Rifkin and Charles Handy say that unless voluntary community service is organised to rebuild communities, we are doomed to crime and violence and a vast outlaw culture. A shorter workweek isn't going to be enough to save civilisation as we know it. Employed workers with more free time on their hands must join with the millions of unemployed to channel the surplus labor cast off by high technology into constructive activity.

That's great advice for industry and government and public policy makers, but why should you do volunteer work? (Besides saving the world.)

Why do men do unpaid, volunteer work?

There are extrinsic rewards, day-to-day, down-to-earth satisfactions in volunteer work such as:

1. Collaborating and cooperating with others to accomplish a goal

2. Producing tangible results you can see and touch

3. Adding variety to your life, not getting stale, bored, and boring

4. Learning new job skills and building up job experience which are transferable

5. Advancing to higher levels of responsibility and complexity within a voluntary organisation

There are also intrinsic rewards which are more internal and personal such as:

1. Meeting new people and making new friends

2. Feeling that you are contributing to society

3. Giving expression to your special abilities

4. Getting the pleasure of enhancing other people's lives

5. Having a place and the means to solve problems and be creative

Steven Barker (Chapter 8) volunteered at the Citizens Advice Bureau so that when he interviewed for a job he could say he was occupying himself constructively even though unemployed. Lawry Rhodes (Chapter 4) pays his dues directing local theatre productions so that he can try out for what he prefers to do, act. Stephen Tharpe (Chapter 29) goes to the West Indies to give financial advice to London Transport retirees, not just to add variety to his holidays. Tony Osmond (Chapter 18) helps run one of the main school orchestras in Hampshire as another way of expressing his love of music.

Gift work, like a job, has to be gone after. Nobody knocks on your door and offers it to you. Probably its greatest personal benefit for men still hoping to find work that pays, is the training you get for work that pays. For example, Chapter 24's Sam Ampem will undoubtedly find his counselling experiences useful when he gets back to teaching and dealing with the problems of today's troubled teenagers.

Chapter 24

Sam Ampem, By Way of Russia

I enjoyed meeting so many determined older people. Many were pensioners who did not need a degree to work, or to change careers. I would ask them, Why are you doing this? Personally, I want a career change, to become a teacher instead of an engineer. They said they didn't want to sit at home watching telly, it wasn't testing their brains. I also enjoyed meeting my tutors. Tutors I respect because they have gone through so many things I'm hoping to go through. Yet they were so humble and modest. Working with us, eating with us, associating with us like ordinary people and making us feel they were one of us.

Sam Ampem, 35, dark-skinned with a black hair and beard, was born in Ghana and is a citizen of Ghana. His father was a journalist, his mother still is a trader. He is engaged to Yvonne from the Netherlands and together they have a long-range plan of returning to Ghana where he will be a mathematics teacher and farmer, and she a nursing assistant. Currently Sam works as a freelance land surveyor. He came to the UK in 1987 with eight O-levels, A-levels in maths, physics, and chemistry, and a degree in mining engineering from six years of study in Leningrad. When we talked he was due to receive his OU BSc focused on mathematics in June 1995 in Wembley Stadium.

Your reasons for doing a university degree?

After my mining degree I worked underground for one year, in the Ukraine, but the poor air quality and the dangers were such that I decided I needed to work above ground. So I came to London and studied land surveying from 1987 to 1991 and got my qualification through the Royal Institute of Chartered Surveyors. During that period I worked on the Docklands Light Railway Development Project, Canary Wharf. The contract was up in 1991 and only then did I realize that surveyors are the very first in a recession to be laid off. I have applied for so many jobs and I know I'm qualified, at least enough to be shortlisted because I have a final pass in the exams of the Chartered Surveyors, yet I'm not shortlisted. I get the feeling that most people who apply for jobs are qualified, even overqualified, but with so many applicants, the opportunity even to be interviewed is limited.

So I decided to study mathematics which has been my hobby throughout my school life. Because I had to work and couldn't go back to full-time education, I did it through the OU. I had watched so many television programs about it, seeing students involved in summer schools and group activities, I was very interested in having those sorts of experiences.

What obstacles did you have?

Working as a freelance surveyor, I used to come home from work late, have something to eat, and then sit down until two in the morning, reading my books and doing my TMA assignments. Finding time was very difficult, and so were finances. Initially I did overtime at work but I had to give it up. I thought, being a mathematician, my studies would be very straightforward, but the pressures of work, my volunteer duties, my social life, made it very tough. But there was no way I was going to let my work or finances stop me from getting that degree. I went to every tutorial, I never absented myself.

I did everything that was required, but unfortunately, I had only two summer schools, and I couldn't join all these groups that go walking on the hills because I was working. Most of the students I met joined these clubs. I wish I could have joined a mountain climbing group because I love to go out in the country and walk in the forests. That's why I want to be a farmer really.

Luckily for me I was able to finish in three years. Because an obstacle for many people is the prospect of spending six, eight years to get a degree. Particularly for people whose studies are motivated by career purposes, they can go to a polytechnic and do a day-release course and get a certificate or diploma within a year or two and do what they want. Seven years is too long for someone who needs a qualification to work. I missed out on my PGCE course because I didn't have the degree yet, that all important paper in my hand. Telling them I had studied for three years wasn't good enough.

How have your studies changed you?

It changed my aspirations for the future. When I met those old people at summer school, I realized that most of them had a dream of going to university when they were young and for a variety of reasons they couldn't. But now, at the end of life, they were going to achieve that goal. Some of them had studied for ten years. It inspired me that people can set a course for themselves, at any age, and achieve.

It also improved my ability to cooperate with other people. I used to ring friends, other students, and we shared ideas on the phone. I used to ring my tutors. I've been able to acquire that quality of sharing ideas, giving opinions, and listening to other people's opinions, and making friends along the way.

What's been the impact of your studies on your career?

It means once I have my PGCE I can teach mathematics at secondary level. I like doing mathematics very much. On my job I am always called upon to help with any calculations. I tend to be the best mathematician in the group. My surveying work is very sporadic and when I am off work, I go around people's homes teaching mathematics. It's easy for me because in my country after you finish your A-levels you have to do national service for one year, which I did for three because I really enjoyed my service job as a teacher at the secondary level.

What's the most important use you make of your degree?

It's made me a better communicator. It's something we acquired through group studies. The tutors gave us the chance to go to the board and explain concepts to the other students. And they taught us to listen to other people's ideas and opinions without interrupting. Their basic idea was to share and give and take. Even if what the person is saying makes no sense, you're not supposed to stop the person. You have got to listen to the end before you put forward another opinion or idea. And you'd never, never say, what you're saying is rubbish.

What are your educational plans?

First, I want to get a Post-Graduate Certificate of Education so I can become a teacher. I hope I get into King's College. Then, after my PGCE, I'd like to get an honours degree in mathematics. Yvonne and I have talked about the future many times and we have come to the conclusion that eventually we will live in Ghana, because when I retire, I would like to be a farmer. The best time to start is not when I am very old, but when I'm heading towards my pension age, say fifty. So we'll go back then and start with the farming. I want to have a palm plantation but there would be cattle and I would also grow maize and plantains. I would go on teaching and Yvonne would carry on with her career as well.

How has continuing your education changed your ideas about work?

Before doing the degree, all I hoped for was to get job satisfaction and security as an engineer. I got some job satisfaction, but not very much, and no security. And over time I realized that my years as a teacher during my national service were the most brilliant years of my life. I still meet my past students in this country and, while I don't recognise them, they know me and they call me by my name. I ask them, what are you doing? Most of them tell me, we are engineers, doctors, nurses, midwives. There they are, the fruits of my labor showing in a very specific way. They're showing me what they are, big men and big women, in society. For all those years I worked on the Canary Wharf project, all those beautiful buildings, they don't tell that you as a person worked on it. But as a teacher, seeing students in professions, coming out successful, gives me the kind of job satisfaction that I really desire.

Living in comfort wouldn't be bad, but money isn't everything. I only want enough to live on and achieve what I want as a teacher and farmer. Success to me is being able to achieve those two dreams.

How did your studies affect your interests?

More and more I like reading about people rather than reading fiction. Biographies about what other people have gone through help me feel I can make it. Many successful people have gone far worse situations than myself. People's profiles help me feel that whatever I set my eyes on, I can achieve that, provided I don't stop, because they didn't.

I also feel an obligation to help other people. I'm the research officer and a counsellor for a charitable organisation, the Ghana Welfare Association. I give advice and counsel to people who have found themselves in this country as refugees. Two million or more Ghanians live outside the country and one thing we're fighting for is to be able to vote absentee.

I constantly attend seminars and conferences which have anything at all to do with immigrants, so that I'm able to give advice to members of the Association who need to deal with immigration, welfare matters, housing, unemployment, benefits. We have our offices in Leytonstone, that's where I have my office hours Tuesdays and Thursdays. I arrange for a welfare officer or a solicitor from the Association, or from the outside, to represent anyone who has to go to the Home Office for interviews on legal matters. And if somebody gets in trouble with the police or the authorities, I find somebody to deal with the matter. I also get information from people like politicians in Ghana on what is happening in the country. I've also got myself involved in many political organisations but all of them legal.

Many people come to me complaining about racism but I tell them there's nothing we can do about it. We are just living here, it's not our country. We must live peacefully among the people here because we can't change them. The best thing to do is to adapt to the situation and live with it.

Why are men reluctant to take traditional women's jobs, for example, teaching part-time in a primary school?

I don't know, because I would do it. Teaching primary, that would be just fine, because I'd be doing what I like to do. If you want to work today, you've got to be flexible. When I was a student, I was a shelf filler, a really low-level job, but I'll do anything I have to do. I don't call any work `women's work.' My traditions and culture are different from here, so that may be the reason I can adapt. In both my country and Russia, there was nothing like a man's job. When I worked in the mines, there were women working alongside men. So many doctors, pilots, are women. In Russia, there is no such thing as a man's job and a woman's job. And in my country, the same thing, a woman can do anything.

Men should change their attitudes and realise it's a changing world. Men no longer are born to be dockers or steel workers or coal miners. Society now needs men to do different work from what they used to do. They've got to be able to work in hospitals and schools, as well as on the shop floor, in what they consider soft jobs, women's jobs. It is no longer a matter of what men were born to be. And men should share the work about the house. When Yvonne and I are married, we'll continue like we do now, sharing everything equally, doing everything together. First of all, we are career-oriented people and she's not going to stop her nursing any more than I would stop my teaching. We aren't going to have many children. If we have any, two will be maximum, because with two we can devise a way to cope with them and also pursue our careers.

When I said goodbye to Sam, he was looking forward to owning a new two-bedroom house in Beckton where there would be more space for his extensive keyboard and stereo equipment and the profusion of green vines and tropical foliage that had the run of the little living room of his council flat.

Chapter 25

New Ideas About Work

Why did I want to go on a course for adult care minders? First, I thought that I could work well with elderly people. Second, I knew that if I did reasonably well on the course and my work placement, I stood a good chance of developing an alternative career. I also knew that once I did that, it would be down to me as to how far I went. Even without a social service qualification, the scope is fairly large.... Care is a rapidly growing profession. I can only hope that there will be more courses such as this one— firstly because it was aimed at an identifiable area of need, secondly because there is a whole army of people who want to work and thirdly because it is an effective method of selection (Leahy, 1994).

Here are a couple more new ideas about work. I haven't yet mentioned the 'phantom promotion'. This is when you get a new and very important-sounding but completely meaningless job title— rather than the raise you were expecting. Or 'creepback', when employers who make over-enthusiastic redundancies are forced recruit new staff on the sly. Or, if you work for the NHS, there is the 'negative patient episode', meaning the patient has died.

But no more about flattening, dehiring, rightsizing, recurving, skill-mix adjusting, or even negative patient episodes. This chapter is devoted to one principle that means jobs for men— go for any occupation NONtraditional for men. Go after any job traditionally held by women.

'What?' you say. 'I read in Chapter 5 that teachers, social workers, and nurses were among the most stressful jobs possible and now you're telling us to go after these jobs?'

Yes. When you think about it, women's traditional jobs are not only available now, they're never going to go away. You cannot automate all of teaching, nursing, and social work. There are always going to be waitresses, beauticians, cleaners, and playground supervisors. Women's jobs are the last preserve of 'a job for life'.

First idea, nursing

Independent headline: `Nurses' numbers down 50,000 in five years.' The number of midwives around the country dropped as much as 22 per cent in the five years to 1994, while the number of nurses in training has fallen by more than 19,000, almost a third. Intensive care units for dangerously sick children can't be opened because there are no specialist nurses to staff them (Hunt, 1996).

Second and third ideas, teaching and care minding

Another *Independent* headline: `There's one hell of a crisis out there.' This time it's teachers. A staggering 50 per cent increase in the number of teacher-training places is needed by the year 2,001. Educationalists do not see how the numbers can possibly be reached given the trickle of applications for PGCE courses in 1995. Applications for specialist teacher training, where already there are shortages, are down 43 per cent in physics, 27 per cent in maths, 25 per cent in chemistry, and a whopping 63 per cent in craft, design and technology from a year ago. Half the teaching force is between ages 40 and 45, and with pressure from local authorities to retire by age 55, these folks are on their way out—when there have never been so few teachers under thirty. The government aims to get the needed bodies by increasing part-time, distance learning routes to certification and by aiming recruitment at people who can't afford to give up their current jobs. Teaching is clearly an area of opportunity for men, especially since there's such a great need for teachers of physics, maths, chemistry, and craft, design and technology (Hodges, 1996).

Then there is adult care minding. Brian Leahy, age 57, quoted at the chapter's start, said his 13-week course exposed him to training consultants whom industry would have paid £1,000 a day, they were that good. Members of his class came from all walks of life including graduates with psychology degrees. His `Adult Care Training Project' was funded by the European Social Fund, run by the Oxfordshire County Council Social Services Department, and was successful in getting jobs for students while they were still students.

A fourth idea, secretarial jobs

Less than one per cent of secretarial staff are male, according to Reed Employment, when many clients are specifically asking employment agencies for men. A temporary secretary, Peter Moore, was a soldier for seven years and served in the Gulf war. He then taught mountain survival at an outdoor centre, so he looks more like a nightclub bouncer than a keyboard operator. After he moved to London to be near his girlfriend, he taught himself typing on his home computer and his agency provided further training. His ambition is to be an office manager or run a secretarial service from home (Saunders, 1996).

Paul Fee made the conscious decision to become a top secretary and in fact ended up a finalist for the 1995 Office Secretary of the Year award. Mr. Fee has been a secretary since 1991 when he left the RAF in which lots of men know how to type. He works for the Bath Mental Health Care NHS Trust as a personal assistant and, like Peter Moore, considers being a secretary a great career path to something higher. Office Angels, an agency which handles a wide range of businesses, says over 17 per cent of its placements are now male, for both full-time and temporary positions (Jones, 1996).

Men challenge for right to do `women's work'

More than 40% of complaints lodged with the Equal Opportunities Commission are now from men trying to win jobs traditionally held by women. Many complaints are from middle-aged men who have been out of work for years. Take Loui Gizzi, 46, from Rhyl in North Wales, who was made redundant from the merchant navy and trained as a clerical worker but was then turned down for an office job. `There's no reason why clerical work should be regarded as women's work,' he says. `But I think executives like to be surrounded by attractive young girls.' Alan Hubner, 28, former bus driver, applied for a £90-a-week job at a model factory in Carlisle but was turned down when he wanted to participate in a subsidised child-minding scheme for his children. The industrial tribunal ruled in his favour. Companies aren't getting away with advertising jobs as only for women, and when they do discriminate against qualified men, they don't get away with that either (Hymas & Thomas, 1994).

David Gildner, Chapter 26, is an activities organiser for a senior citizens centre in Aylesbury. He used to be a machine operator and did his first university course simply to prove he was as good as the men who supervised him.

Chapter 26

David Gildner, Outdistancing the Eleven-Plus

Impromptu she dances, on her own

but not alone,

holds conversations with the clouds

and shouts at the rain.

Introducing long forgotten ghosts,

whose names she remembers,

while forgetting her own.

Marvely, a word with no meaning

that tells of the past.

Asleep in an instant

to dreams of reality,

she wakes with a start

and cries for no reason

and then laughs at the fuss.

Marvely, strange words with no meaning

that tell of her past.

This poem by David is titled `Edith'. I met Edith and took away a photo of her smiling, holding David's hand. She is one of his Alzheimers clients at the Hartwell Day Centre in Aylesbury where he has been Activities Organiser for six years. His eyes were bright blue and his cheeks pink from the harsh December weather when he arrived at the station in a windbreaker, black trousers, and comfy lavender shirt, its pockets stuffed with notes and lists related to his work.

David was born in 1946 in London into a working class family. He left school at fifteen with no qualifications and very poor school reports. He started the OU in 1986 and got his degree in 1992. He is married to Susan, who is the administrative manager for a private nursing home. David was diagnosed as having multiple sclerosis in 1990, which he is only now considering a disability as he gets more easily fatigued. Continuing education is his lifeline beyond MS.

Your reasons for doing a university degree?

I've always had semi-skilled engineering jobs since I left school. The firm I worked for was a manufacturing firm, they made parts for machinery, and they employed skilled, semi-skilled, and unskilled workers. And I always thought I was as good as the skilled workers. So I did it out of bravado, especially by starting with an art course. If anyone had expected anything of me, it would have been that I would study technology. I thought, No, I'll go completely the other way. I only wanted to wave a piece of paper at the people I worked with on the shop floor, and say, Look, I've done this.

I was never going to do anything in engineering. I hated it, but it was a job and I thought that was all I was capable of, without an apprenticeship or the right qualifications. At that age I wasn't going to go any further and if things got worse, I was getting to an age where I'd get offered less skilled jobs.

What obstacles did you have?

Leaving school at fifteen with no qualification, I would describe myself as almost illiterate. My father was ill so instead of being at one school for a long time, we moved all over the country. I went to three secondary moderns. For his last twenty years my father was disabled, he had emphysema through working in industry, so we moved from one sanitorium to another. I really don't remember much about school except that it was a bad experience for me. I was always in the bottom stream. The eleven-plus was a disaster. I went in knowing that I didn't have a chance.

So before I started my studies I took a six-week evening class first. Basically what they did was get you to write a couple of essays. I was terrified. All along I was thinking, Oh, these people, they're better than me. I've always had a hang-up about my written work, grammar, spelling. I'm the world's worst speller. But I quite surprised myself. My essays were okay. Then when I started on the course there were thirty people at the first tutorial and I was overawed. Never said a word. In fact, I don't think I said a word the whole year.

And at the end of the year was the exam. First I thought I wasn't going to do it because I'd fail. But somebody was able to read my script. I got eighty per cent. That decided me to go on and started the idea that I could use my studies at work. I'd always wanted to get out of engineering. I had this hazy cloud that encompassed social work, so I did the social science foundation course and all my credits since then have been social science.

How have your studies changed you?

That first year I was running on fear. My expectations, other people's expectations, were that I can't do this. The first thing I got out of it was self-confidence. My first tutor realized it was my first stab at doing anything academic and her remarks on my essays were so good, that I've gone back to them since, whenever I was struggling and needed encouragement.

And I had another tutor at summer school, to look at him, he looked like a homeless, scruffy little man, with this Manchester accent. But when he read poetry, I discovered something I really cottoned on to. I read poetry now, which I never would have done, and I also write it. It gives me a sense of achievement to get something written every week. People have said, why don't you show it to somebody, but it's still like sitting in the back of the class and not saying anything.

One of the things I used to be quite well known for when I was in engineering was I was bolshy. I had lots of heated rows and then I wouldn't speak to the boss for days. I was filled with animosity about conditions, but I couldn't articulate it. I'm still argumentative about what I see as inequalities, but not in such a destructive way. I can talk an issue through and make a good case for whatever.

The course that helped me most see things differently was State and Society. New terminology, new ideas, a philosophy that I found quite hard. But it also gave me more confidence in my ability. Now if I set myself a task or an objective, I don't go into it like the eleven-plus, thinking I'm not going to pass. I can give anything academic a go now and am confident that I can do it.

Two years into my degree I started reading employment ads in the paper. I applied here for the experience of the interview. To my surprise, I got the interview and I got the job. I put down on the form that I was studying for a degree and my boss was doing the OU herself, so we spent a lot of time talking about our courses. I'd never done this kind of work before. But somebody working on a shop floor who was going home with his dirty fingernails every day and studying? That's impressive. Plus to the question of why would you be good at this work? I said I could empathize with the generation of men who come here, a lot of whom have worked in factories.

What's been the impact of your studies on your career?

Before them, if someone asked, could you work in this setting, I would have said no. That's not me. I'm an engineer. I wear overalls. I couldn't work in a place like this.

I also use my courses here at work. That room I showed you, the special needs room, I got that off the ground, and it's got quite a high profile in social services. The idea is that daycare should move towards small groups within a centre. Like that program for the severely handicapped that has a better staff to client ratio so you can give them more time. And, while we have group activities, we work with each client as an individual, whether it is arts and crafts or board game or memory game. The carers all say they've observed improvements in their relatives from the stimulation. The way I've made a success of it is by recognizing the needs in individuals. Like a lady who has Alzheimers and they couldn't do anything with her at home, she wouldn't speak to anybody. We found that she had been a midwife and run a home for unmarried mothers, so we got her involved in reminiscence work using pictures of babies. The local paper has a column every week, New Arrivals, with pictures of babies, and we'd get her to give us her views, which one is the prettiest baby? The liveliest baby? And her son rang us up and said Mum came home today really high, talking and talking about babies.

What are your educational plans?

My planning goes back to when I was diagnosed. I had to sit back and think what it meant. I knew quite a bit about it anyway, because we have clients here with MS. I thought, should I give up my studies? Do I need to give up my studies? Will I be able to do it? Am I going to be in a wheelchair? And I thought if I can actually carry on studying and I have got MS, having a degree will be a help. So it was a lifeline. I applied for a field social work job and although I've got the qualifications, I never even got an interview. I asked my boss if MS was a factor. She said they shouldn't really do that. So I applied for more or less the same job, different team, and got the interview. But I was getting worse and I didn't carry through with the interview because I thought I couldn't physically do the job. I have trouble myself going shopping, and taking clients shopping with me, it's not fair.

It's one of the reasons I'm pursuing an honours degree. My first course ties up with my work here, Community and Personal Life Histories. I'm happy here, but there's no promotion ladder. So, I ask myself, is this it? Is this my final job?

How has continuing your education changed your ideas about work?

In the old days success was bonus pay. The harder you worked, the more you'd get. Now success is when a client's carer rings up and says thanks. We've notice a big change in Mother or Father. We're grateful for what you've done. As far as redundancy goes, it is not helping our stress levels that Buckinghamshire is going through a reorganisation of the county. We don't really know where we're going or whether our jobs are safe. There are people being interviewed in that room down the hall this morning for their own jobs because we have to reduce our staff from twenty to eighteen.

Personally, I'm philosophical, because money is no longer the be all and end all. I've got a degree. It's a safety net. Whatever happens, it happens. I know that sounds sort of hippy, sixties, but I'm not really worried.

One thing that's hard for me to imagine, though, is using the degree at the management level. It goes back to this eleven-plus thing, that's still there. Other people have said that I could do management but....

What was most important in your life before and after the degree?

I used to play squash and football and I liked watching soccer. The football was Sunday morning stuff for the local territorial army team. The standard was pretty dim, but we did it for the social side of it, a few beers. Squash as well.

You might say what was important was going out for a beer on a Friday night and standing there lusting after the barmaid. The stereotype of boys out on a Friday night was my world, that and football. I still go out on a Friday night but people say I'm not one of the lads anymore, and that's okay. I don't really want to be one of the lads anymore.

Studying and work are most important now. I get quite involved when I'm at home preparing things for my job. The MS thing is very important to me because I want to carry on working as long as possible. Also I read a lot of poetry, I quite like the modern poets, the Liverpool poets. Roger McGough, Adrian Henry, Peter Powell. And some who are not with us anymore. Sounds pretty boring, doesn't it?

Why would you recommend continuing education to other men?

Because it sets things in motion. I'm sure other men are like me. When I was in industry my inability to communicate was a problem. I was angry about what I saw as injustices, but I couldn't articulate or explain it. Now I can, but I can also stand back and see lots of different points of view. It's not black and white, us and them. That's how you change. Whereas before on a Sunday or a Friday when I went out with the boys, had a drink, whatever we were talking about there was a good way and a bad way of doing everything. Take hanging. You either hung 'em or you didn't. You were for it or against it. Now, like everything else, I have to stand back and look at it from different perspectives.

I'm good at one-to-one work with clients and staff, and in groups of three or four, my views and ideas go down very well. But in big groups I'm still very quiet. I will sometimes not speak until I'm asked, What do you think? My boss keeps asking, What can we do to bring you out? I've seen members of staff go on courses in assertiveness training and public speaking and seen the changes in them. So I've got the opportunity to work on this problem which is very frustrating to me.

Some of our clients are ex-teachers and they try to talk me into teaching and I say, No, I'm too old for that, but the real problem is no way could I stand in front of a class.

Why are men reluctant to take traditional women's jobs?

They have a Them versus Us mentality, a Male versus Female mentality. If I see people I used to work with, they make facetious remarks about my work. The male-female thing is quite deep-rooted. Take whistling at women from building sites. I wouldn't do it but I understand why men do it. That sexist attitude is everywhere, it's still in the family, it's everywhere at work. I work mostly with females here, my boss is female, but some men who work here have the same attitude toward women as men who work in industry. They don't put up page 3 pinups, but if they could, they would. Attitudes haven't changed that much, attitudes like the woman's place is in the home and men should be the providers and put the tea on the table.

Before I did my degree, my friends were exclusively male. I've got close friends now that are female, that I work with, and my wife and I socialise with, go to the theatre with. I wouldn't have done that before. Most men wouldn't. They see women primarily as sex objects.

At my second summer school, I got quite friendly with a girl who was ten years younger than me and we'd go off and talk about the course, went out for a meal a couple of times. That was it, a friendship, nothing more, but when I recounted this to the boys, they didn't believe it. That we could have gone back to her room or my room, at two in the morning and that was it. You go back to a woman's room, it's got to end up in bed. We didn't, and I got ribbed about it.

Tell me about the state of the elderly in the UK today.

They're getting a bad deal. The dominant government view is it shouldn't be society that looks after the elderly, it should be the family or local community. But society is such that families are split up and moving constantly all over the country. Extended families don't live and work in one community like they used to. Sons and daughters move away, mothers and fathers are left on their own. The government wants people to be mobile, that's what our economy depends on. Many elderly left on their own in communities can look after themselves if they have enough money. But they have to be assessed regularly by somebody who says, for example, `You do need a nurse to come and give you a bath. It's our responsibility to provide that to you as a citizen. We're all citizens of the United Kingdom and we should all be entitled to a basic set of rights and if you can't provide for yourself, it shall be provided for you.' That means society as a whole should provide it. But the will is gone and everybody's supposed to stand on their own two feet.

One of David's other poems, `Public Enquiry', ends with these lines, `From silver tongues, "Community, rationalisation, empowerment", as from the back of the room unnoticed, unheard the question is whispered "who really cares about us?"'

Chapter 27

Lifelong Learning

One of the more moving moments of my life was watching a degree ceremony at Britain's Open University. It was held, appropriately I thought, in a cathedral because each graduate was there because they had made an effort toward some form of personal renewal.... Grannies were there, and great-grandfathers, photographed by their progeny in their caps and gowns with their degree certificates, instead of the other way round. There were people in wheelchairs and others with guide dogs. Age was no barrier in that place, nor class, nor creed, nor colour, nor previous success in anything, for it is a truly `open' university (Handy, p.196).

It's impossible to run the gamut of opportunities for lifelong learning here, so now a hint of the wide possibilities in addition to the Open University.

The National Extension College

Founded in 1963, it was the model for the OU set up in 1969. The NEC offers more than 150 distance learning courses and has 30,000 students worldwide. It provides courses in basic literacy, numeracy, language and computing skills. It offers GCSE O- and A-level courses and professional qualifications for the Engineering Council, Institute of Linguists, and Institute of Marketing. It also provides distance tuition for University of London degrees in a number of subjects (Schofield, 1997).

Successors to Britain's first community university

Which is the Community University of the Valleys in South Wales. It offers students from mid-twenties to late sixties a five-year, part-time BA degree in modern Welsh studies, modern European studies, and environmental studies. How-to-study sessions run alongside lectures, teaching how to take notes, identify vital information, and structure essays. David Thomas, 41, is a typical student. He's a former miner who has survived a heart attack and now does environmental studies while his children are at school. He doubts he can put his degree to practical use in that locality, but `It's not so much what I can do with a degree, but what a degree course is doing for me now' (Road, 1994).

'Fast track' study makes the grade

Pilot studies at ten new universities have found mature students taking fast-track, two-year degrees are as likely to pass as students in three-year programmes. The 69 per cent overall pass rate among students on accelerated courses was one per cent higher than the rate for regular courses. This was true for business administration, design, engineering, science, education. Going fast track makes especially good sense for mature students since they are more likely to be hired at graduation because of greater practical experience (MacLeod, 1994a).

One guinea pig was 42-year-old Ken Gibson who ran away to sea when he was sixteen and had never sat an exam in his life. With no academic background to speak of, he finished a fast track humanities degree at Nottingham Trent University and was headed for postgraduate work. Nottingham's special programme didn't lose a single mature student to panic attacks or financial problems which the University was afraid would happen in this unfamiliar, highly pressurised school environment (Meikle, 1994).

The Open College

If you have heard of the Open College, you may think it is as another further education version of the OU. But it isn't. The Open College gets no money from the government. Its original purpose was to publish teaching materials for distance and open learning for FE institutions. But now its clients are corporations such as Marks & Spencer, Ford, and Abbey National who buy courses in management/supervision, technical training such as process operations, health and care. The way individuals can tap into the Open College is by talking employers into buying their materials and then signing up to do the course.

Another way, if you want to study management, is through the Open College courses for individuals. These last from three months to two years and employ standard distance-learning techniques—self-contained texts and workbooks and tutorial support over the phone. Most management courses involve a project which you can do at work, if you're in work, or at a voluntary organisation if you aren't (Pritchard, 1996).

Other forms of corporate training

Tesco calls their two-year management training programme for university graduates, Excel. Half of those on the scheme have not come straight from university. Mature graduates can complete the programme in less time. Tesco doesn't insist that you've studied any particular area. What they're looking for are people with drive and ambition who can get on with others and handle responsibility (Trapp, 1996).

Ford's training programme is exemplary. The Ford Employee Development Assistance Programme (EDAP) is not job-related. Instead, employees can take courses in just about anything—literacy, numeracy, foreign languages, underwater photography, losing weight, stopping smoking, learning to drive.

Ford gives employees £200 a year to study and employees submit applications to committees of management and union reps for approval. Over half of Ford's 30,000 UK employees have taken part. The company also promotes an Automotive Engineering Honours degree, trains 800 apprentices, and puts 2,500 engineers through an Engineering Quality Improvement Programme that teaches team work which is replacing single-task production line labour (Fisher, 1994).

Postgraduate studies

Some employers say people with a higher degree will get the job over an applicant with a first degree. There are in Britain more than 11,500 full-time and part-time postgraduate research and taught programmes lasting six months or more. They are listed in printed directories and on the Internet. Eleven per cent of 1994 grads continued further academic study, and another eleven per cent entered postgraduate vocational courses in teaching, social work, the law and other professions (Schofield, 1996).

If changing is really learning

`...if effective organizations need more and more intelligent people, if careers are shorter and more changeable, above all, if more people need to be more self-sufficient for more of their lives then education has to become the single most important investment that any person can make in their own destiny. It will not, however, be education as most of us have known it...the old British notion of education as something to be got rid of as soon as one decently could (Handy, p.168).'

Seventy per cent of all jobs in Europe in the year 2000 will require cerebral skills rather than manual skills—public service, data processing, social work, science, music, computer software, banking, post and telecommunications. One half of these brain-skill jobs require the equivalent of a higher education or a professional qualification. By Handy's calculations, some 35 per cent of every age group should today be entering higher education. Only in Japan, the US, Taiwan and South Korea are university populations of the right size for the future.

Of course, of course, of course, the government should be doing something about it. But it isn't, and even if it started doing something tomorrow, you can't wait. You have to take responsibility, sole responsibility, for your continuing education.

Two men's stories before the wrap-up. Ian Flintoff gives us his ideas about when education and work should occur in our lives, and Stephen Tharpe puts Ian's ideas into practice, as well as Handy's idea that older people, rather than leave the workforce, should become part-time assistants to younger people.

Chapter 28

Ian Flintoff, Actor, Politician, Scientist

You can never go to an OU summer school without seeing this amazing cross-section of society. The first time it brought tears to my eyes, the beauty of it, seeing these people arrive, some 80-odd, some late teens, a total mix of social backgrounds, the sexes, ethnic groups. It was as if some inspired educationalist had realized that real education is the overall view of society as a whole. I was in an all-male college at Oxford which was mainly Etonians who were charming people, but I can't kid myself for a moment that Trinity College had anything of the majesty or poetic brilliance and imagination of the Open University. The Open University is a century or two ahead of Oxford.

I'll bet that's him, I said to myself, when I spotted a trim man with close-cropped brown hair, dressed in the sombre colors of winter, dark green, navy, and gray, bending forward to examine close-up enlarged black and white photos of memorable casts and performances.

It was ten in the morning and we climbed the staircase to the top level of the National Theatre to do the interview in a deserted foyer, with the clatter of catering and maintenance staff stacking coffee cups and replacing lightbulbs in the background.

Ian is 56 and began his acting career at the age of 22. He is married to Deirdre, a solicitor, and they have three grown children. He began the OU in 1989 concentrating in science, got his BA three years later, and is now taking ecology to finish his BSc honours degree. Ian was born in Preston and went to a grammar school that required three O-levels (his were Latin, English, and mathematics), followed by three A-levels (French, Spanish, English literature). He learned Russian at Cambridge during his three years in the army, after which he went to Oxford to study languages for a year.

Your reasons for doing a university degree?

I moved into it stage by stage. I didn't know, to start with, where I was going. I'd always had a whimsical interest in wanting to understand the physical and the chemical reality of human beings. It fascinates me that inert matter becomes human, that I could eat a tomato and it would become part of my body. I started with the science foundation course—physics, chemistry, biology, and earth sciences—and focused narrowly more and more as time went on towards biochemistry and the biological sciences. I don't think one can really be an actor in the most rounded sense without having familiarity with the concepts and ideas of contemporary science. Politics and the arts have been marking time while science has moved on.

In this country everybody is worried now about the per cent of the population in retirement by the year 2050. This shows that the biological sciences have been leaping ahead. Their job is to extend life, mitigate illness, alleviate suffering, and they've been filling their brief. But the politicians and sociologists haven't kept up with them; they're still thinking in 19th century terms. Instead of worrying about who's going to pay for all these pensions, why not think how do we get an income and an input from people between 60 and 80? Some technology should now be being investigated to harness the skills, wisdom and experience of over 60-year-olds who want to work between 60 and 80. It could be done with computers, working from home. With modern technology and 50 years to go, we could find a new workforce whose usefulness would be inconceivable.

What obstacles did you have?

My only obstacle has had entirely to do with my erratic work pattern. For example, most of the subjects I've done perforce have demanded summer laboratory experience. And that means that somewhere like March I've had to say, on the first week in August I will be at York University doing biochemistry. Now as an actor, the precarious job it is, I don't ever really know in March if somebody's going to say to me, Will you come and play *Hamlet* that weekend? So every single year, I've kept my fingers crossed. The year before last I had to switch it. The job did coincide so I had to get on the phone and say, Can you excuse me the first couple of days? I'll hare off as quickly as I can on Sunday morning. So I did two *Hamlets* on a Saturday, one at 1 o'clock and one at 6, at 11 o'clock finished, rushed home to Fulham, had supper, set the alarm for 6 o'clock, and drove up to York, so I could catch up as quickly as possible.

It has meant also that sometimes I haven't been able to go to tutorials. But my tutors were always extremely kind to me, very encouraging by letter and telephone. They'd arrange tutorials in central London and say, Could you come at 8 o'clock in the evening, and I'd say, Yes, yes, I'll come for the whole year, and then something turns up and the hours clash. You can't excuse yourself as an actor to the boss and say, I won't be in tonight, because if you're not there, there's nobody playing your part.

How have your studies changed you?

Exactly in the way that I wanted it to. I wanted to be able to see human beings and human affairs from a hill on the other side of the valley. The timing is related to the fact that I stood for Parliament in 1987, in Plymouth, for the Labour Party against David Owen. I was deeply unhappy about the way I felt Britain was going so I decided I would get out of the political armchair for once and do something. I let the constituency know in 1985 that I was interested. I'd done some political work before, I'd been a councillor in Kensington. But I'd never been in Plymouth in my life. They asked me to go to a selection meeting and so I made a speech and I was surprised I got through the first selection. Then they sent for me to go back for a second one. Anyway, in 1985 I got the nomination.

After the election in 1987 I realized I had got so involved in the world of talk, language, speech, words on the stage here or words on the platforms in Plymouth, that I wanted to get down to something dispassionate, objective, rigorously clinical. That's why I started studying.

What's been the impact of your studies on your career as an actor?

There might be a small degree of extra confidence. Darwin made a great impression on me, as are the big debates that are going on now, about what the reality of evolution is. Once you get excited about that, you can never look at a human being again, whether on stage or off stage, in quite the same way. We are a pretty dynamic animal. It is a shattering thing to be a human being. So in the sense that I see those things now which I was blind to ten years ago, it gives me an added, extra confidence.

Actors should be able to play parts that demand a scientific understanding. Now the plays, perhaps, have not been written. The world is now so importantly developing along the lines of the biological aspects of science that writing should start to be done that concerns itself with these issues, therefore, actors will be needed who can handle the material with confidence. It will need a new kind of actor who can articulately, poetically, and adventurously deal with the new problems that human beings face through science. For the future it should be an essential part of the actor that he comes from a scientific background.

What's the most important use you make of your degree?

I've started writing. I've had one or two plays produced in the last three years, one at the Edinburgh Festival. One was called *Mind the Gap* which was a political farce done in London in two fringe theatres, in Battersea and Wood Green. The other one was called *The Magpie*, which was done at the Edinburgh Festival for six weeks and at a theatre called the Dock Theatre, Duke of Cambridge, Camden, for a month.

And I write articles in the papers, mainly about the interface between politics and the arts, and recently letters, in a very crude way, about the philosophy of science. I had a few letters in about the `selfish gene'. My point was that a metaphor like `the selfish gene' begins to cloud the issue because you're personifying genes with human attributes, because genes don't have brains, appetites, ambitions. So the very title of the book I find suspect. It's graphic but it's dangerous. Scientific language has to be different from the language of Shakespeare.

And I hope I'm a better actor. I like to confront the public in that way. Preferably with people like Shakespeare, although I was phoned last night about the possibility of doing Arthur Miller for the first time, which is something I would leap at with more zeal than I can possibly tell you. He's capable in characters like Willy Loman of making characters of Shakespearian magnitude and it doesn't surprise me in the least that *Death of a Salesman* and *The Crucible* can be transposed to any culture or society around the world and have, as the people of Japan or Nigeria feel, enormous relevance.

What are your educational plans?

The idea of doing a thesis for a PhD is not completely out of my thoughts. If I were to get a good enough degree and people were willing to discuss it with me, I wouldn't mind finding some way of writing a thesis over five or six years. Bringing together the role of science in politics, the arts, a rounded society. It's not the popularization of science. That has been tried and doesn't work. That leads to a most entertaining *Jurassic Park*, or the glib bits of journalese you see, in the national papers, A New Cure for Cancer, or We've Cracked AIDS. It needs to be a real input into the people's understanding, in which, therefore, they can call to account the politicians and the administrators. And the arts play an important role in this. I can't even think of a title for such a thesis yet, but I can see it in a cloudy way.

I certainly feel like a scientist when I put that hat on, yes. When I discuss with scientists, when I think about scientific concepts, when I read scientific books. And it has crossed my mind to take a year's leave of absence to do research if somebody persuaded me that if you went out for a year and did something very deep and intense in a scientific way, you could pick up when you came back...but the economic and social status of actors is so wobbly, you get very neurotic. Some actors go to America to try their luck and come back, and they've lost both. They didn't make it in the States and here they're forgotten.

How has continuing your education changed your ideas about work?

There's too much pressure on young people. `I've got to get a mortgage.' `I've got to make a million by the time I'm 25.' It wouldn't be a bad idea to have a young person's pension during which time they can achieve a maximum of education, until the age of 30, and after that work. I think youth should be a time of happiness, a certain amount of carefreeness and exploration.

We should somehow make sure that young people have that sort of economic exploratory freedom. And the world of science and politics has become so complex and complicated, to get the barest fingerhold on it, I think takes until 30. Then between 30 and 55, we could probably have something more or less as it is now. And then there should be the moment of choosing. If people at 55 or 60 feel that they want to work on, then technology should be applied to enable them to do so. Those who feel that they can't or are unable to work any longer, a similar system should apply as applies now. They are given enough financial and economic support, but should have the opportunity to take up employment and education again, if they wish to. I see no limit to that. If somebody's going to live to 120 and decides at 110, It's time I got my act together now because I've wasted the last century, then he should have the opportunity.

As far as success is concerned, lots of people with fairly high peaks in their careers don't deserve them, because in too many areas of importance, including science, they are more ignorant than they should be. And many people whom I would regard as successful, including the scientists I learned about, get no support from anybody at all. They can do research for years at their own expense and no one hears of them until they win the Nobel prize. There are hundreds, if not thousands of scientists, in this mold. So my studies gave me a different set of values of who is deserving of the accolades of success and who is undeserving.

What was most important in your life before and after the degree?

My wife is the most important thing in my life, it goes without saying. But it doesn't go without saying! Happiness with that particular woman is the paramount thing in my life. But if I set aside my private, domestic life, acting was and is certainly the most important thing to me, finding good plays, doing good work, and I still enjoy very much the discipline of acting. I think there should be a national service where everybody should be an actor for two years. It teaches you about truthfulness, it teaches you about what's happening with other people. You can't be on stage without being in tune with the audience. You can see their fear when a line goes. You can tell when somebody's doing a line without truthfulness. It means when we listen to politicians talk, actors can spot a million miles away that there's deadness behind the eyes here. This is phoney.

It brings you right down to the meaning of words, communication, the rigor of training, rehearsal, picking away at a text. And if you're picking away at something like Arthur Miller or William Shakespeare, you're picking away at somebody that's going to teach you a hell of a lot by the time you go on stage a month afterwards and deliver it to an audience who admire you and are always rooting for you. I'm one of these actors who loves the first night because I can't wait to join them. Many actors hate audiences, some pace up and down on the other side of the curtain, swearing and shaking their fists. For me, it's the other way round.

Why would you recommend continuing education to other men?

I had no chemistry at all, yet I was able to take on concepts that I had never been engaged with before at the molecular, biochemical level. I put the credit, though, to the course and the tutors, because if I needed elucidation of any kind, stumbling in the dark, they made it clear to me. I did just one maths thing and that was to brush up a bit because I'd never done calculus. I found I got so much pleasure from doing these abstract mathematical calculations that when I'd finished and done the exam, I was getting up in the night and going down to the kitchen to do calculus as a relaxing, mental exercise. It's almost the same kind of pleasure you get from a good coffee, the immediacy, the reality, almost tangible. It's the ordinariness of the experience that is so agreeable.

We have got an extraordinary brain and just as fish gotta swim and birds gotta fly, human beings have to use their own evolved mechanisms. It's the brain that made us what we are, the most wide-spread species on the globe, the only species that's ever been responsible for its future evolution, the only species that's responsible for protecting its own predators. We look after the lions now. And the exercising of that faculty is nothing particularly special. Its ordinariness is like the running of the gazelle or the flight of a bird. We just happened to have evolved this particular thing.

What the educational system, plus the harrowing economic present, are doing to young people today is impossible to express in words. I see young men now in groups on street corners, terrified but bluffing it, who can't talk to women anymore, who have sadly lost all possibility of real communication with a young woman. Partly because of the way they as men are depicted in the media. I try sometimes to conjure myself into other minds. I see somebody on a street corner, and I think, I want to think exactly as you do. And when I've thought of the bleakness of, say, being 20 and there's no light, not even a candle in the near future, of any kind of job. Now think about having a home and a wife and children? It's just preposterous.

There are people who say, Well, these young men are probably better off not marrying, better off not having children, and women are probably better off not having them as husbands. Such writers are pulling whole pillars out from under evolved humanity, and saying, We know better. But I've not heard any substantial evidence of a scientific, moral, or artistic nature, that persuades me that this sanctioning of the changed order of things, the young men on the street corner, the women on their own, is for the best. It took hundreds of thousands of years to get to this point. That's why I feel that the kindly enlightened people in science, politics, and the arts must somehow get together and stop this crap, which is going to hurt the next generation and the ones after that. A man and a woman is some crude form of mutual comforting, after all, and it also leads, at its best, to enormous creativity and imagination.

An actor's job: temporary, short-term, insecure, erratic, unpredictable, wobbly, ill-paid. But, like all jobs, one that needs continued education to bring the most to it.

Chapter 29

Stephen Tharpe, Systems Union Handyperson

When Stephen came round our flat for lunch in February 1995, he carried with him an overflowing briefcase which contained his voluminous writings and files, photos and poetry. He chuckled over a snapshot of himself as Father Christmas at a benefit children's party with a little girl who, after announcing that he couldn't possibly be Father Christmas because he was black, wouldn't leave his side. The occasion was the inspiration of the poem at the end of this chapter.

Stephen was born in 1934 in Jamaica where he did the Junior Cambridge examination and the Senior All Schools Certificate. He came to the UK in 1955 and began working for London Transport in 1956, retiring from his position as group station manager in 1992. Seven months later he joined Systems Union, a software company, for five hours a day as a handyperson. He and Editha, who told her story in *OU Women* have five children, ranging in age from 21 to 34. He began the OU in 1977 and got his BA in 1983.

Stephen's chapter is not so much about the impact of continuing education on his early career, as upon its impact on his Third Age lifestyle—writing, traveling, counselling, connecting with relatives and friends.

Your reasons for doing a university degree?

I'd always wanted to have a degree, but the high school that I attended wasn't one of those whose goal was to get its students into university. At my private, small high school, you did your school certificate and then you got a job. But having come to England, I thought I'd like to do my degree and when the opportunity arose, this was partly due to Editha giving me a push, she said shall we do it, and we both applied.

I had done other courses. I did a diploma course in personnel management by correspondence. I also did the Chartered Institute of Transport course. It was when I was a junior in the administrative grades of London Transport because it was always so much easier in an interview when you were asked, what are you doing to better yourself, to be able to say, Well, I'm doing the Chartered Institute of Transport course. With that, your interviewer would recommend that your salary go up.

What obstacles did you have?

I'll just tell you a little story. At first we tried to study at the weekend if Editha was off. We'd set everything up at the dining room table to do our studies and the children would be in the front room watching television. And one time we had just sat down and there was this yell and one of my sons had fallen and cut himself just above the eye and the blood was gushing out. We had to take him to the hospital to get stitched and when we came back, we decided we would never, never again work on the weekends. Weekends would be free for the children and from then on, we only studied during the week.

My study time was from eleven o'clock at night til three in the morning. I had to wait until the children were asleep. Then I would wake up at six. And this has dogged me ever since, because I can't get out of the habit. I've tried very hard but I still go to bed at three. One o'clock would be early for me. The other thing that happened to me with all that reading, is my eyes have never been the same.

What was the impact of your studies on your career?

When you do distance learning, you have to be very self-sufficient, work things out on your own. So I learned to look at problems by myself. My mind got trained to look for what's important. I learned to scan reports very quickly and pick up the points I needed. It definitely helped me get my promotions from the administrative grades to the executive grades and eventually into the management grades. After that first arts foundation course I focused on social science courses that would help me in personnel management.

Tell me about your new job.

I saw it in our local paper. Five hours a day looked nice, so I applied. A handyperson does anything, setting up their filing system, making sure maintenance work is done around the place, making sure pictures are put up properly. Furthermore, the company has the perfect holiday scheme for me. Every year they pay for you and your spouse to go away on holiday for a week. They have a winter holiday in April, this year to Vancouver, and a hot holiday in October, this year to Kenya. Editha and I are hoping to go on that one. The staff goes together. I actually was offered another job thirty hours a week with a building society but it was a sales job, like so many firms nowadays. Even when I worked for the Underground, our new image was sales, go out and get clients, get people to use the Underground, which we'd never done before.

Tell me about your writing.

My studies gave me a love of writing. My tutors would say things like, `You've got a way of expressing yourself,' and when you get this sort of encouragement you go from strength to strength. At first it helped at work, both my writing reports that got to the point, and helping my managers to write brief, concise reports. Because I myself learned to do it that way.

Then when I was working at Finchley, it took me forty minutes to get to work and forty minutes to get back in the evening, so I started scribbling, mostly about my childhood, Jamaica, my family. I write poetry as well. And as I went along with it, it got better and better. It took off for me. There are times at work when I'll scribble a poem and put a little piece of paper in my pocket and go home and have a look at it and finish it off and type it up on my computer.

I'm writing a book I tentatively call *Harroplain* because that's the family's name, Harrop. It's a book of fiction, based on my life. I've probably done 150 pages. I'd like to get it published at some time. Here's a poem that got published. Here's one about committing suicide on the Underground. And here are certain things that I wrote for my children's school. And here I'm writing about setting up a newspaper stand. After I retired from London Transport, I set up this *Evening Standard* pitch at the Ravenscourt Park station. When I worked at Finchley, if I didn't buy my paper when I left there, when I'd get to my station, I'd have to make a detour to buy a paper. I decided if I ever had the time I would set a paper stand up. I got up the courage to ask a guy in a petrol station how to go about it and he gave me the critical contact number. I started selling papers in December but before that I went around the station and put up little notices, `Soon you can get your paper here.' But in '93 I went to Jamaica for six weeks and I had to get someone to stand in for me, and again when I went to Barbados. I thought this is really tying me down too much. But there was a guy who sold flowers there and he took it over. And now they've got an automatic machine, would you believe, that you can buy your *Evening Standard* from.

This is a talk I gave to some pensioners last Christmas. And here is `The Battle of the Rush Hour', something I wrote for the school magazine. And this, `The Lady in White', is about the ghost at Archway for the Archway magazine. And here's something I wrote in *The Pensioner*, a local newspaper. And this article is about a program in Hammersmith. Editha and I go out with handicapped people, we push their wheelchairs. And this certicate is for giving a talk to the Rotary Club of Montego Bay.

What's it like to go back to Jamaica?

When you go to a black country, there's a certain lack of stress. When I get off the plane in Montego Bay, I feel very relaxed. I can't say why really. But when people leave here to go back to live in the West Indies, not all of them end up that happy. I've visited London Transport pensioners in Jamaica and in Barbados and they all have a problem because they are considered different. Not different in colour, but different in outlook. These pensioners were unhappy because they weren't being told what the rate of exchange was for converting sterling to dollars when their money arrived. I'm the West 6 area representative for London Transport pensioners and because I was going to the West Indies I said to the manager, if you give me a list, I'll see if I can sort this problem out.

So I went to the banks and they would say, `These people` have an attitude. They think everybody should jump when they speak.' The people who work in the banks think of them as English, and disregard them. I can understand this, because even though I spent twenty impressionable years in Jamaica, I then spent forty years here, and when I go back, it's not easy to ditch the last forty years. When I was in Jamaica a friend came to see me and my brother who lived down the street. This friend didn't arrive until ten o'clock and insisted on calling on my brother. We went to his house and it was obvious he'd gone to bed so I said there's no point in disturbing him. And this guy says, No, we'll call on him and he knocked and my brother got dressed and we all went out together. I would never have called on someone at that hour but that's my attitude here. There my brother would have said, Why didn't you call? It was only ten o'clock.

How did your studies affect your interests?

When I was studying, I did not have time to get involved with the student body. Coping with home, job and studies didn't give me much time to go to things in the evenings and Editha worked nights. But once I graduated, I thought, now's the time and I've worked ever since with the graduate body. I was chair of London's Graduate Association for five years. We organised local social events and we tried to get into the decision making of the University. But when I became manager at Finchley, I relinquished the chair but remained on the committee so I could have my input. Then I was on various committees setting up the national graduates association which was formed in 1987 and I'm now the regional rep for London graduates.

My education course brought up certain inequalities in the school system that normally you don't think about. It made me want to see what the ethos of my children's school was and what their integration problems might be so I became a school governor. And I've been a school governor ever since. My children all went to Fulham Church of England schools and I worked in the parent-teacher association in those.

But when my job moved to Finchley, it was impossible to visit the Fulham schools which I felt was necessary, just to walk around and see what is actually happening. So I took up a governor's position in Barnet. I was with Livingston

School and St Margaret's nursery, which have the same management. This was fine, because the management of London Underground encourages you to take part in local activities, so it was also my contribution to this local community. And after I retired, I was co-opted as a governor at a primary school in the north of the borough, Kenmont. The course made us really want to help, to improve things, to make an input.

Did your education course have any impact on your relationship with your children?

Yes, because what happened to my children in primary school was that the teachers had no expectations for them. The children got on well together, they had many friends, still do from then, even though the only black children in the primary school were mine, so St. Peters certainly didn't reflect the makeup of society. I'd go to the school for their reports and the teachers would say, Your children are very nice and they're working to their ability. And I'd say, What do you mean, to their ability? No answer. And I'd ask, What do you expect of them? No answer. One of my sons stopped working at one time and Editha spotted it, looking at his maths homework and they were all wrong. She said, That's not right, and he said, Well, it doesn't matter because my teacher never looks at it anyway. She was always too busy and put him off. The fact that we were able to spot it at an early stage and talk to the teacher, that helped.

It also helped that when Mom and Dad said it's homework time, that we also had homework. It gave them extra incentive. It was like going to church. We used to send them to church, but at times we didn't go. And when they got to a certain stage, they totally rebelled and said if we're going to church, why don't you come? So we had to go to church as well.

One thing I wished I'd learned about children is when to push. I would think, if I push, am I going to push them over the edge? Will they do something silly or stop working altogether? So I didn't push too much. I remember my daughter, her teachers said she'd do fine at university, she was very good at languages, and she came one day and said, Can I have a break? And then I'll go and do my university. She had her break but she's never been back. So, should I have said no at that stage? What would have been the result? Would she have continued and worked hard? One son now is on the MBA program at the OU. Editha's picture and my picture at graduation are in the sitting room and he said to me, Dad, I'd like mine to go there. Another son wants to start at the OU as well, he's just had his papers through.

The problem for young people today considering university is, they think, what am I going to do when I finish my degree? If I leave my job now and go to university, what will I come out to? They don't have the prospects we had. We could see openings, we could follow other peoples' examples. We could say, I'll go to university because I want to be this, or that, and we could be. But now, whatever you decide on, it's likely you'll have to change to something different.

It sounds like you do a lot of traveling now.

Well, in 1993, Editha and I went to Jamaica for six weeks. And we went to Spain for a week and we spent a day in Tangier. We also had several trips down to Romney where we bought a chalet in 1992 and we went to Tenerife because I've got a time share there. I also went to Barbados for four weeks with a cricket team from London Transport. My next door neighbor came along so I had company. And right now we're looking forward to our hot holiday in Kenya in October. It's such a good company. We have such fun. We had a table tennis tournament not so long ago. I was runner-up in the finals so now everybody wants to beat me.

Now, from a notebook on the Underground:

Who'd be Father Christmas in this day and age?
My letters tell of unemployed with so much righteous rage.

The festive season gives them pain
As their children all expect again,
Those wondrous toys that last year brought,
But which are merely this year's anxious thought.
I run this empire on my own,
Covering continents and towns.
I try to keep their spirits high,
Despite the darkened, hidden sky.

Perhaps if I could share the job,
A lot more people would have jobs,
And letters would be much less sad.

I'll try this tack for the coming years,
To help these parents dry their tears,
As they brighten up their children's year.

Chapter 30

The End of Work?

If you draw an angled line between Bristol and the Wash, you divide the country into two halves with roughly twenty-seven million people on each side. Between 1980 and 1985, in the southern half they lost 103,600 jobs. In the northern half in the same period they lost 1,032,000 jobs, almost exactly ten times as many. And still the factories are shutting. Turn on the local television news any evening and at least half of it will be devoted to factory closures (and the other half will be about a cat stuck up a tree somewhere....) So I ask again: what do all those people in all those houses do— and what, more to the point, will their children do? (Bryson, 1995, p.167)

Experts say we have maybe thirty years until two per cent of the world's current labor force will be producing all the goods necessary for total demand. The European reaction to the disappearance of traditional manufacturing and low-tech jobs can't last forever, that is, keeping salaries high and social services generous. Nor can the American strategy of keeping salaries low and cutting back poverty programs. But how to handle the global employment crisis is for top Summit goers. Your own crisis is enough for you.

The men you have got to know here decided to cope by continuing their education, indefinitely. Their university degrees were a step along that way. Now's the time to summarize the benefits of that education when it comes to working in the 21st century.

Complete career change

For five men the degree meant they changed their careers completely. Lawry Rhodes went from building society manager to secondary school English teacher. Eugene MacLaughlin left teaching business studies at the same level as Lawry to become a lawyer. Steven Barker's redundancy from a job as a paint technician led to a career as a professional social worker, and David Gildner's semi-skilled engineering job was supplanted by a position as daycare activities organiser for the elderly. When he has his teaching qualification, Sam Ampem can quit being a freelance surveyor and teach his beloved mathematics.

Overall, these career changes show several important characteristics. They all moved to higher-level work in terms of qualifications, responsibility, and complexity. There is also a shift away from traditional masculine work and toward traditional feminine work. And a shift towards greater job security in terms of today's job market. And while we didn't talk money, my bet is they are making, or will make, more money after than before.

But the changes that most impressed me were their heightened job satisfaction (anticipated in Eugene's and Sam's cases) and the stimulation their new fields of interest provide them. David goes home and immediately starts thinking up new exercises for his charges. Lawry is caught up in student play productions as well as productions for the adults of Greater Bexhill. Sam goes out and tutors math in neighbors' homes until he has his own classroom. And all five men now possess confidence that they can continue to change and move ahead.

Promotion

Five men got promoted up the ladder because of their degrees, George Saint and Stephen Tharpe within London Transport/Underground, Michael Moore within the AMI Priory Hospital, Edgbaston, Raj Ragiwala within BT, and Jim Bailey within Marathon Petroleum. George's and Stephen's promotions seem pretty straightforward management moves. Raj's and Jim's promotions, however, were both up and over, into new, more complicated activities, forecasting and systems analysis. And Michael's nursing career keeps expanding in all manner of directions.

Everyone interviewed agreed that a university degree gives a man an extra edge within any organisation when it comes to decisions about who to move up or over, who to keep and who to let go. All other things being equal, the man with the degree, the man who continues to improve himself, has the advantage. Even if the degree is not directly relevant to the job. Because it says something about his character.

Enhanced careers

Who felt they were better at their job or retirement, regardless of what the job or retirement consisted of, and regardless of how they were better at it? All of them.

I'll never forget Raj turning an imaginary object around in his hands as he talked about gaining a never-take-anything-for-granted perspective on the world. Nor can I forget Lamber's premonition that it would be a good thing to learn as much about computers as possible, and fast. And how his job continues to change every year and how he could never keep up if the degree hadn't taught him how to manage his time and learn on his own.

Then there is Michael who as a teenager was told by his careers master that his head was in the clouds if he thought he could work with computers. Now, just when the nursing profession needs it, he's into computers in a big way and sorting out other people's technical problems. And who'd think biochemistry would help deliver Shakespeare? But Ian got so excited about science that `you can never look at a human being again, whether on stage or off stage, in quite the same way.' So that, yes, the degree gave him a degree of extra confidence and the background actors of the future will require.

Extra confidence is the common denominator of career enhancement. But it isn't just outer confidence to suddenly take on new, unfamiliar tasks and responsibilities. They also have a palpable inner confidence in the face of on-the-job stresses. They don't get riled up anymore. They face uncertainty with equanimity. They have learned a job is not the be all and end all.

Thriving retirements

At age fifty, Peter Bolton didn't really want to stop being a pilot but he wanted out of Britannia Airways. So he applied to Saudi Airlines and `I have reason to believe the degree was looked upon favourably by the personnel officer at my last job interview and may have helped me get the job offer: he was keen to have a copy of my academic record for my file.'

Mahmood Tootoonchian retired early from Irano-British oil shipping to begin, at age 48, a lifelong dream, a degree in psychology. His retirement is now filled with continued study, translating articles, travels and friends. He says the degree was all gain and gave him a chance to develop personally, and he seems indeed a very contented man with a full round of intellectual and social activities.

After 33 years as a disgruntled British Telecom engineer, Tony Osmond would have liked to use his degree to teach but couldn't fight the 55 age limit. Nonetheless, he has taken another job, like the one at BT, `just a job,' unconnected with his higher education. But that education taught him a little bit about a lot of things and, most importantly, brought him into contact with someone to share them all with.

But perhaps the retirement par excellence is that of Stephen Tharpe, who has done what Charles Handy recommends in the Third Age, taken a job as an assistant in his specialty to younger professionals. Management was Stephen's area of expertise and, how appropriate now, that he is the handyperson part-time for a small corporation. He is aware of the big picture as he goes about doing little tasks to make the work environment pleasant and smooth-running. Just as important are the too numerous to mention volunteer activities Stephen's immersed in. But then a large portion of his life has always been devoted to caring for others in the community.

The hallmark of these retirements is contentment. Contentment based on having accomplished a big goal, on achieving academic success, on having developed old and new interests, and on appreciating one's homelife and partner.

Preparation for nonpaid work?

All the men are carrying on studying. All of them have developed new recreation. They travel more now. They are taking up sailing and acting and geology fieldtrips and learning foreign languages. But despite their concern about men who might never work again, men who will never work period, young men with no hope of wife and children, elderly folks freezing in their homes, children emotionally deprived by their parents—as a group they are doing remarkably little about these social problems.

This result of my `study' might be worrisome to Charles Handy and Jeremy Rifkin. They have called for the private and the public sectors to get the voluntary sector funded and organised, like yesterday. But, again, what's an individual to do until industry and government get their act together? Well, a body's got to act. On his own. Especially if he agrees with Jeremy Rifkin's analysis.

`We are entering a new age of global markets and automated production. The road to a near-workerless economy is within sight. Whether that road leads to a safe haven or a terrible abyss will depend on how well civilization prepares for the post-market era that will follow on the heels of the Third Industrial Revolution. The end of work could spell a death sentence for civilization as we have come to know it. The end of work could also signal the beginning of a great social transformation, a rebirth of the human spirit. The future lies in our hands (p.293).'

The challenge for lifelong education is to expand students' visions of work to embrace gift work, the only form of work which is truly unselfish. Every man reading this book could do more to sustain the community, the community of his choice, at the same time that he pursues study work to sustain himself. I do not believe there will ever be an end to work.

References

Aitchison, Cathy (1995) Jacks and Jills of all trades. *Independent*,
    2 February, p.30.
Ashdown, Paddy (1996) Everyone needs a second chance. *Independent*,
    30 January, p.15.
Boseley, Sarah (1994) Old disease made acute by family and job changes.
    Guardian, 17 November, p.3.
Bryson, Bill (1995) *Notes from a Small Island*. London: Doubleday.
Caine, Naomi (1996) Women bring home the bacon. *Sunday Times Money*,
    3 March, p.3.
Caulkin, Simon (1994) The workplace revolution. *Observer*,
    25 September, p.6-7.
Cooper, Yvette (1996) Sir Ron must solve the 16-plus education riddle.
    Independent, 1 March 1996, p.23.
Daniel, John (1991) The Open University in a changing world. *Open Learning*,
    6, 3-8.
Delgado, Martin (1996) 1 in 2 British marriages now `doomed to fail.'
    Evening Standard, 20 February, p. 14.
Donegan, Lawrence (1994) Pension fears add to family burden. *Guardian*,
    8 August, p.2.
Driscoll, Margarette (1994) The unmarriageable male. *Sunday Times Section*
    2, 13 November, p.6.
Driscoll, Margarette (1996) Mind the age gap. *Sunday Times Style*,
    3 March, p.8.
Fisher, Paul (1994) Some degrees of coercion. *Guardian 2*, 3 March,
    pp.14-15.
Garner, Clare (1995) Two incomes, one child, no time. *Independent*,
    26 October, p.4.
Hadley, Katharine (1994) Worried sick by work. *Sunday Times Style*,
    20 November, p.27.
Handy, Charles (1995a) *The Age of Unreason*. London: Arrow Books.
Handy, Charles (1995b) *The Empty Raincoat*. London: Arrow Books.
Harnden, Toby (1994) In the name of the fathers. *Guardian 2*,
    9 August, p.12.
Hodges, Lucy (1996) `There's one hell of a crisis out there.' *Independent*
    Section Two, 25 January, p.22.
Hunt, Liz (1995) Mature students `outsmart' young contemporaries.
    Independent, 20 December, p.7.
Hunt, Liz (1996) Nurses' numbers down 50,000 in five years. *Independent*,
    18 January, p.4.
Hutton, Will (1996) *The State We're In*. London: Vintage.
Hymas, Charles and Thomas, Lesley (1994) Men challenge for right to do

`women's work'. *Sunday Times*, 20 February, p.11.

Jones, Helen (1996) Be nice to the secretary, he could be the boss one day. *Independent Section Two*, 25 January, p. 27.

Kingston, Peter (1994) Better late than never. *Guardian Education*, 21 June, pp.4-5.

Leahy, Brian (1994) Training for a life of care. *Times*, 11 August, p.6.

Leathley, Arthur (1994) Britain's workers `sick men of europe'. *Times*, 2 June, p.10.

Lord, Graham (1996) Can Penguin swim against the tide? *Evening Standard*, 17 January, p.54.

Lunneborg, Patricia (1994) *OU Women: Undoing Educational Obstacles*. London: Cassell.

MacErlean, Neasa (1996) Down and out Britain. *Observer*, 17 March, p.1.

MacLeod, Donald (1994a) `Fast track' study makes the grade. *Guardian*, 28 April, p.11.

MacLeod, Donald (1994b) Time to target the boss. *Guardian 2*, 3 March, p.3.

McKie, David (1993) Nations in a state. *Guardian 2*, 1 December, p.10.

McRae, Hamish (1996) You can't treat a skill-force like a workforce. *Independent on Sunday Business*, 3 March, p.4.

Meikle, James (1994) Life in the fast lane. *Guardian Education*, 21 June, pp.2-3.

Moore, Suzanne (1994) The private life of the public servant. *Guardian*, 11 February, p.5.

Moyes, Jojo (1995) Long hours culture hitting productivity. *Independent*, 26 October, p.4.

Mulgan, Geoff and Wilkinson, Helen (1995) Fast forward. *Guardian 2*, 6 June, pp.2-3.

O'Kelly, Lisa (1994) Lonely life on the British treadmill. *Observer*, 31 July, p.21.

O'Sullivan, Jack (1996) Keep young and employable. *Independent*, 9 February, p.15.

Parker, Ian (1994) The feel-bad factor. *Independent on Sunday*, 18 December, p.4.

Peters, Tom (1994) Dropping old anchors. *Independent on Sunday*, 1 May, p.20.

Pritchard, Stephen (1996) Open to a new way of learning. *Independent Section Two*, 11 January, p.15.

Pye, James (1991) *Second Chances: Adults Returning to Education*. Oxford: Oxford University Press.

Rifkin, Jeremy (1995) *The End of Work*. New York: Jeremy P. Tarcher.

Rifkin, Jeremy (1996) Now the robots are after your job, too. *Independent*, 26 February, p.11.

Road, Alan (1994) Mining new wisdom. *Observer Review*, 23 January, p.25.

136   References

Rowlands, Barbara (1996) The new British disease. *Independent on Sunday Magazine*, 3 March, p.68.

Russell, Willy (1991) Foreward. In James Pye, *Second Chances: Adults Returning to Education*. Oxford: Oxford University Press.

Saunders, Bill (1996) Take a letter Mr Brown. *Independent on Sunday Real Life*, 11 February, p.7.

Schofield, Paul (1996) Reasons to be a postgrad: 1, 2, 3. *Independent Section Two*, 29 February, p.14.

Schofield, Paul (1997) Any time, any place, anywhere. *Independent on Sunday Business*, 12 January, p.12.

Sex equality. *Guardian 2*, 18 November 1992, p.11.

Sieghart, Mary Ann (1994) The incredible shrinking career. *Times Magazine*, 1 October.

Smith, Jane (1994) Who cares about men? *Guardian 2*, 15 August, p.13.

Smith, David (1994) No jobs for the boys but girls are doing fine. *Sunday Times Business*, 16 January, p.3.

Stepney, Rob (1996) Being male means being mortal. *Independent Section Two*, 8 January, p. 3.

The war between the sexes. *The Economist, 330*, 5 March 1994, pp.80-81.

The manufacturing myth. *The Economist, 330*, 19 March 1994, pp.91-92.

Timmins, Nicholas (1996a) New man fails to make it into the Nineties. *Independent*, 25 January, p.5.

Timmins, Nicholas (1996b) Quarter of men jobless after they reach 55. *Independent*, 22 February, p.7.

Tooher, Patrick (1996) The boss is demoralised, downsized and delayered too. *Independent*, 16 September, p.3.

Trapp, Roger (1996) A super market for the ambitious. *Independent Section Two*, 25 January, p.27.

Value of a Mum. *Legal & General Report*, September 1996.

Watson, Shane (1996) Stress, panic and you. *Evening Standard*, 20 February, p.24.

Weir, Patrick (1994) King of sweet nothing at all. *Independent II*, 9 February, p.21.

Wilkinson, Helen (1994) Slackers may be tomorrow's winners at work. *Guardian*, 30 November, p.26.

Woodley, Alan (1988) Graduation and beyond. *Open Learning, 3*, 13-17.

Index